# SWEAT EQUITY

What It *Really* Takes to Build America's
Best Small Companies—
by the Guys Who Did It

## GEOFFREY N. SMITH
## PAUL B. BROWN

SIMON AND SCHUSTER
New York

*109*
*MC 8286✓*

Copyright © 1986 by Geoffrey N. Smith and Paul B. Brown

All rights reserved
including the right of reproduction
in whole or in part in any form
Published by Simon and Schuster
A Division of Simon & Schuster, Inc.
Simon & Schuster Building
Rockefeller Center
1230 Avenue of the Americas
New York, New York 10020

Designed by Irving Perkins Associates

Manufactured in the United States of America

1   3   5   7   9   10   8   6   4   2

Library of Congress Cataloging in Publication Data

Smith, Geoffrey N.
Sweat equity.

Includes index.
1. New business enterprises—United States—Case
studies.   2. Success in business—United States—Case
studies.   3. Entrepreneur—Case studies.   I. Brown,
Paul B.   II. Title.
HD62.5.S625   1986       658'.022       86-6622
ISBN 0-671-55210-4

To Anne Christine, without whom . . .

—P. B. B.

To Sweet Pea

—G. S.

# Acknowledgments

Entrepreneurs can't do everything themselves and neither can two writers trying to put together a book on the people who have built the best small companies in America. We needed the help of a lot of people to get the job done.

The help came in many forms. First, from the entrepreneurs themselves, who were extraordinarily generous with their time.

From the Forbes organization, notably Malcolm and Steve Forbes, and James Walker Michaels, who, in suggesting the creation of the Up-and-Comers column, introduced us to emerging growth companies.

From Stephen B. Shepard of *Business Week,* who was understanding of the time it takes to put a final manuscript together.

From Alan J. Zakon, chairman of the Boston Consulting Group. His insights into this field are exceptional and we used his thoughts—especially in our discussion in Chapter 4 of how to spot an opportunity—as a jumping-off point.

From our editor, Fred Hills, whose thoughts about how to organize the material proved invaluable.

From Kiril Sockoloff, who first suggested the idea of turning what we had learned into a book, and from Connie Clausen, who made that thought possible.

From Anne Bagamery for her unerring sense of geography, and Barbara J. Rudolph of *Time,* who offered numerous suggestions that made the book better.

And from our families, who made it easier to put this whole thing together.

# Contents

## CONTENTS

**6**

# The Players

1. APOLLO COMPUTER, Chelmsford, Mass.
2. BRENCO, ball bearings, Petersburg, Va.
3. CPT, word processing equipment, Minneapolis, Minn.
4. CONAIR, health care products, Edison, N.J.
5. CRAWFORD & CO., insurance, Atlanta, Ga.
6. DREYER'S GRAND ICE CREAM, Oakland, Cal.
7. HEALTH-MOR, vacuum cleaners, Lombard, Ill.
8. HUNT MANUFACTURING, office and art supplies, Philadelphia, Pa.
9. *INC.* magazine, Boston, Mass.
10. INTERNATIONAL CLINICAL LABORATORIES, Nashville, Tenn.
11. KINDER-CARE LEARNING CENTERS, day-care centers, Montgomery, Ala.
12. LOU-ANA FOODS, Opelousas, La.
13. METEX, automotive supplier, Edison, N.J.
14. MINNETONKA, personal health products, Minnetonka, Minn.
15. MOLEX, electronic connectors, Lisle, Ill.
16. NAUTILUS, health and medical equipment, Latana, Fla.
17. OAK INVESTMENTS, venture capital, Westport, Conn.

18. OSBORN MANUFACTURING, metal finishing products, Cleveland, Oh.

19. PALL CORP., filters, Glen Cove, N.Y.

20. PAWPRINTS, greeting cards, Jaffrey, N.H.

21. PLENUM PUBLISHING, New York, N.Y.

22. POSTAL INSTANT PRESS, Los Angeles, Cal.

23. REEVES TELECOMMUNICATIONS, New York, N.Y.

24. RIVAL MANUFACTURER, household appliances, Kansas City, Mo.

25. SAFECARD SERVICES, credit card insurance, Fort Lauderdale, Fla.

26. SAFEGUARD INDUSTRIES, paper and computer supplies, King of Prussia, Pa.

27. SAFETY KLEEN, cleaning solvents, Elgin, Ill.

28. SEAGATE TECHNOLOGY, disk drives, Scotts Valley, Cal.

29. SEALED AIR, packaging, Saddle Brook, N.J.

30. SHOPSMITH, woodworking equipment, Dayton, Oh.

31. TOFU TIME, Tofutti, Rahway, N.J.

32. TIMEPLEX, Woodcliff Lake, N.J.

33. TWENTIETH CENTURY INSURANCE, Woodland Hills, Cal.

34. U.S. SURGICAL, surgical supplies, Norwalk, Conn.

35. WATERS ASSOCIATES, liquid chromatography, Foxboro, Mass.

36. WELLS GARDNER, video equipment, Chicago, Ill.

37. XOMOX, Teflon-lined specialty valves, Cincinnati, Oh.

# How This Book Can Help You

This book is about what it's like to start up a company from scratch and turn it into one of the most profitable and fastest-growing young companies in the country. The entrepreneurs themselves will do the talking. This is their story, as they saw it, and as they lived it. These are the lessons they have distilled from their own triumphs and failures.

You'll find no buzzwords here. No broad-brush concepts. No thoughts from an ivory tower. What is here is the hard-won practical advice on what to do and what not to do from the men and women who have done it themselves. This book is about the problems you can expect when you stop thinking and talking about starting your own company and actually try to make it happen.

We call this book *Sweat Equity* because it's about the entrepreneurial perspiration that builds value out of dreams. The term originated in the inner city. There, poor families can get a mortgage from the city, if they're willing to put in the time and effort needed to renovate an abandoned home. Their down payment—or equity—is their sweat. Entrepreneurs—who seek their money from banks, venture capitalists or friends—undertake a very similar voyage in building their businesses. In the pages that follow, you'll read about the frustrations, as well as the thrills, of that creative "sweat equity" at work.

If you are already in business, you'll recognize the problems these entrepreneurs faced. As you read about the challenges that confronted them, you may find ways of approaching your own problems differently.

Investors, too, will benefit. Everyone who has bought a stock—or even thought about buying a stock—has wondered how to spot the next IBM. Highlighted here are some of the companies that truly have a shot at becoming giants. And the very entrepreneurs who run those companies will be pointing out the pitfalls along the way to greatness. You'll learn what to watch out for before you invest.

## How These Companies Were Selected

How do you find the best small companies in America? First, start with a definition of small. We believe that any company that has made it to $100 million in sales can no longer be considered an emerging growth company. If sales have topped $100 million, the company is no longer emerging; it has arrived.

But even eliminating all companies with over $100 million in sales still leaves a large universe—98 percent of all American companies have less than $100 million in revenues. To winnow the list further, we applied some basic financial criteria. To be considered, a company must have:

- Maintained an average 15 percent annual earnings gain over the last five years. Just because a company did well in the past is no guarantee that it will do well in the future, but it is a good harbinger.

- Produced an average 15 percent return on equity for at least five years. We figured at this stage of their lives, these companies should be outperforming the 13 percent average turned in by the Standard & Poor's 400 if they are to have a long-term shot at success.

- Achieved that return with debt that did not exceed equity—to eliminate highly leveraged, speculative businesses.

These financial criteria are a good starting point. In any given year, it will produce about two hundred names, and those are the companies you should examine when you are thinking about investing in emerging growth companies.

We started with this list as well. From there we whittled further. We knew from experience that only half the companies that met our financial requirements this year will qualify again next year, and we were looking for those with staying power. Companies too dependent on forces beyond their control—such as the oil and oil service companies—were eliminated. From there, we were more subjective. Companies that weren't unique, such as distribution firms, were eliminated. If it seemed a company didn't have a clear focus—it started as a restaurant chain and just announced it was going to buy a munitions firm—it was eliminated. So were companies that entrepreneurs couldn't learn from. For example, several companies we looked at made one terrific product—developed years ago—and that was all they were ever going to make. Such examples were not too instructive.

But while we eliminated companies that passed our financial criteria, we also included some that failed our tests. Why? Because they illustrate the pitfalls that even the best companies can fall into. Besides, hard-and-fast rules don't spot winners. You have to make exceptions. For example, it is silly to say debt should not exceed equity for companies such as fast-food chains, hospital management concerns, and child-care centers that require a great deal of real estate. Similarly, a company poised for explosive growth may make heavy investment in new equipment one year that could penalize earnings. You have to know when to bend the rules.

We bent them in two particular cases. First, we included a handful of companies such as Hunt Manufacturing and Lou-Ana Foods, even though their sales now exceed $100 million. When these companies were much smaller, they made pivotal decisions that allowed them to break through the $100 million sales barrier. Because they have done so well, we wanted to discuss those decisions.

More importantly, we bent the rules when we met chief executives such as Abe Kraskoff of Pall Corp. or Bill Poduska of Apollo Computer who truly knew what their companies would face as they grew.

## Life Cycle of Emerging Growth Companies

In talking to literally hundreds of entrepreneurs over the last five years, we found, not surprisingly, that their companies had experiences—and difficulties—as different as the people who created and ran them. But for all those differences, when we sat down to see what we had learned, we found the similarities were far greater than the differences.

We discovered all companies—whether they are in soap or software—live through a cycle that looks like this:

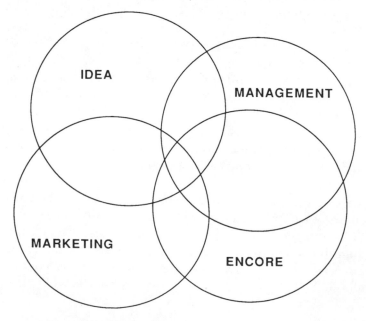

This sketch shows that the four stages of development overlap, and that each is needed to create a company that will succeed. It does you no good to say that you thought of creating a nationwide chain of hamburger stands if you never try to market the idea. If you stop at the idea stage, you'll spend the rest of your days grumbling into your Big Mac.

Similarly, the third circle in the diagram shows that finding someone to buy your idea or product is worthless if you don't make money. Loss leaders may be an excellent way of attracting business, but if that's all you have, the only thing you'll create is work for the bankruptcy lawyers. It is here in the management stage that the idea begins to click. Production costs are controlled, staff is hired, and every product that can be extended is extended. But instead of ending an entrepreneur's challenge, success here leads to its own set of problems. Once you have filled every niche and cut every cost, you have to decide what to do next.

How you go about finding the next idea—the encore segment of an emerging growth company's life cycle—is a process that mirrors the idea phase closely. Not surprisingly, the problems that follow are similar as well.

But while the phases a company will go through are predictable, the progression won't be. As the sketch reveals, the way emerging growth companies proceed through their life cycles is far from linear.

A wonderful idea for a product can be quickly rendered obsolete when the market collapses, as we will see in the discussion about Brenco. Or just when you think your marketing plan is in place, you discover, as Perry Mendel did in starting the Kinder-Care chain of child-care centers, that the idea that seemed so obvious to you is hard to explain to the general public. And so it goes throughout a company's growth. No one phase is ever completely finished. They are all intertwined. The best managers understand this. So should investors.

.  .  .

We found that this simple model—Idea, Marketing, Management, and The Encore—tracks the lives of all small companies. We have used those four headings as the organizing principle for this book. It provides the framework as the entrepreneurs—the people who have built America's most successful businesses—tell you how they handled the problems and opportunities they faced at each point of the cycle. What they did right, and perhaps more importantly, what mistakes they made.

Here, then, is how a small business really evolves and how successful (and unsuccessful) entrepreneurs deal with the challenges they face in growing.

# Part I
# THE IDEA

# 1

# Do You Really Want to Make a Million Dollars? And Other Questions You Are Likely to Answer Wrong

If fate had been different, Martin E. Tash would now be an aging rock star living on an island retreat, instead of a youthful executive working in Manhattan and living in the suburbs.

While growing up in Kew Garden Hills, Queens, in the 1940s, the Tash family lived in a row house that shared a common wall with the Simon family next door. The Simons had a son a year younger than Marty. The boys were fast friends.

"Sports were everything when we were growing up, and we were probably the best two athletes in the neighborhood," Tash recalls with pride thirty years later.

As they became teenagers in the 1950s, the Simons' son developed an interest in singing, as many boys in the rock-and-roll era did. And who would be better to harmonize with than his buddy Marty? "The only problem is I am absolutely tone-deaf," says Tash. "Paul went two blocks away to sing with Artie, who had an absolutely wonderful voice."

Artie is Artie Garfunkel. And so the duo Simon and Garfunkel was born.

But while he is not as rich as Paul Simon, Marty Tash has done well. Tash is now chairman of Plenum Publishing Corp., which publishes specialized—and expensive—books with titles such as *The Fundamentals of Digital Switching*. There are also magazines like *Folia Morphologia, Hyperbaric Oxygen Review*, and the *Journal of In Vitro Fertilization and Embryo Transfer*. Not many people read Tash's publications, so not many publishers want to publish them. (Plenum considers a book a best-seller if four thousand people buy it, and its average magazine has a circulation of about eight hundred.) But if you are a scientist, doctor, or engineer, you have to read Plenum's publications to keep up with the research in your field, and you pay for the privilege. A book can easily run fifty dollars. The average magazine subscription costs one hundred dollars.

Those high prices are part of the reason for Plenum's success. Another is that Tash is . . . well, cheap. For example, when Plenum's New York landlord raised the rent, he moved the company to cheaper quarters on Spring Street, in a slightly seedy part of lower Manhattan. It isn't particularly fashionable, Tash concedes, but he has a ten-year lease at four dollars a square foot versus the fifty dollars he'd be paying in mid-Manhattan, where most publishers have their offices.

When it came time to head downtown, Tash refused to hire professional movers. "I got estimates, and they wanted two hundred thousand dollars. So we hired three workmen for three months, bought a truck that we needed anyway for our warehouse, and did it ourselves for thirty thousand dollars." Tash helped pack the boxes.

Plenum is now one of the most successful small companies in the country. Tash's $40 million (sales) company is always among those at the very top, every time *Forbes, Busi-*

*ness Week,* or *Inc.* compiles a list of the best small companies in America.

Tash clearly knows something about entrepreneurship. And he responds with an interesting question when people ask him if they should go into business on their own.

"I ask if they want to make a million dollars," he says. "Everybody always says yes, but they are answering the wrong question. What they mean by yes is yes, they would like to have a million dollars, a house on the ocean and all that. They don't necessarily want to earn it.

"Having money is nice," says Tash, who drives a luxury Mercedes and keeps a condominium on the ocean in Florida, although he still dresses like the accountant he once was. "But all having money really does is keep you from worrying about having money.

"The hard part is building a business to the point where you have that million dollars," he adds. "But that is also the part that is the most fun."

## Entrepreneurs Are Different

That in a nutshell may be the difference between the people whom you are about to meet and the rest of us. To people like Tash, what's important is translating their visions into reality. That's why they start companies, not to become rich. Wealth is just a pleasant by-product.

---

*Don't set out to be rich. Set yourself a commercial goal and accomplish it. Wealth will follow.*

---

Indeed, if you reverse those priorities and set out to be rich, you probably won't accomplish anything. That's the thinking of Jack C. Massey, and he ought to know. Massey is the man who for $2 million in 1964 bought a small fast-food chicken chain known as Kentucky Fried Chicken.

Seven years later, after increasing sales fourfold, he sold
KFC to Heublein for $239 million. Massey then helped
found Hospital Corporation of America, which now owns
or operates more than four hundred hospitals, and which,
following its 1985 merger with American Hospital Supply,
had revenues of over $7 billion. And with Winners Corp.,
another fast-food chain, Massey became the only man in
the history of the New York Stock Exchange to start three
companies listed on the Big Board.

So Massey, now worth $150 million, clearly knows some-
thing about being a successful entrepreneur, and his advice
echoes Tash's. Don't set out to be rich, he says. If you do,
you will be too impatient to do anything right. Instead, set
yourself a goal and accomplish it. If you do, you will make
money.

The drive that makes people like Tash and Massey accomplish their goals is similar to the drive to excel found in
actors, artists, or athletes. But while different entrepreneurs
have different visions they want to turn into reality, they
all, as we shall see, go about accomplishing their goals in
the same way.

# 2

## It Doesn't Have to Be Original

On College Avenue near Claremont in Oakland, California, is exactly where you would expect to find the Dreyer's Grand Ice Cream Co., a maker of premium ice cream. About six blocks from downtown Berkeley, Dreyer's is across the street from College Square, a small, fashionable mall filled with boutiques that sell everything from stuffed animals to gourmet cookery.

Dreyer's administrative offices at 5929 College are on the second floor of a building of red brick and honey-colored wood. The ground floor is taken up by a Dreyer's ice cream shop, decorated with white tiles and ceiling fans. Cutesy white polar bears are for sale, along with the thirty-two flavors of ice cream.

But while the location and setting are perfect for a gourmet ice cream company, the route that T. (for Thomas) Gary Rogers, Dreyer's chairman, took getting there was anything but. "I would like to tell you I had some carefully planned scheme, but it really was a case of opportunity slapping me in the face, and me being able to recognize it," he says. The opportunity was one that has made Dreyer's one of the fastest-growing small companies in the country. Sales have more than tripled in the last five years while earnings have climbed fivefold.

But Rogers couldn't foresee that kind of success—or even

21

being in the ice cream business—back in 1972. Back then he had a decision to make. A young consultant for McKinsey & Co. in San Francisco, he loved the problem-solving aspects of the job, but wasn't looking forward to making partner. "McKinsey is a wonderful company; I thoroughly enjoyed my time there," Rogers says. "But partners are expected to 'have clients.' That means spending time on the politics of the business, joining the right clubs, maintaining client relationships, and bringing in new business, and I was less interested in that."

But while he knew what he didn't want to do, Rogers was still groping for a way to make his mark. With a partner (W. F. Cronk III, now president of Dreyer's) he started a chain of limited-menu restaurants, similar in concept to Steak & Ale or Victoria Station. But Rogers quickly became disillusioned. "We had a couple that were quite successful in California. Then we opened a couple in Texas that were disasters," he recalls. "We were certainly not on the road to creating the kind of company we had hoped for."

Realizing he was not cut out to be a restaurateur, Rogers started searching for something else to do. Ice cream retailing, then an unsegmented market, was one possibility. So was a chain of parking garages. In his search, he deliberately avoided looking at sexy fields like high tech.

---

*Look for opportunities in industries everyone else is bored with. At least the competition ought to be easier.*

---

Software and other glamorous industries, Rogers quickly saw, were crowded or soon would be. "All my highly educated, bright, fast-charging friends gravitated to 20 percent of the SIC. [Standard Industry Codes, used by the government to classify types of businesses.] Anyone who wants to make a million dollars says, 'Software!' Sure, the demand is great, but since everyone wants to do it, those fields are

oversupplied. To succeed against people who are going to
turn in times of 9.4 in the hundred-yard dash, you have to
run 9.2. That's not easy. Your competition in those fields is
already working nights and weekends, and you have to
work even harder. I wanted something where I could succeed by running a 12 flat."

It wasn't that Rogers feared hard work. You don't graduate with honors from the University of California at Berkeley and the Harvard Business School by merely being glib.
Still, it is a lot easier to run the hundred in 12 seconds than
9.2. So Rogers began looking at the 80 percent of the fields
that most everyone else was ignoring, figuring that even if
success wasn't guaranteed, at least there would be less competition. The dairy industry offered the most opportunity,
Rogers thought. It hadn't changed in eighty years.

That insight coincided with a curiosity Rogers had about
a nearby ice cream shop. And it also meshed with a change
in the buying habits of the people who would become his
market. Everything came together when Rogers decided to
kill some time on a slow Thursday afternoon.

Almost every day, Rogers drove by Bill Dreyer's Ice
Cream shop on College Avenue in Oakland. Dreyer's ice
cream wasn't cheap. But the quality kept the lines long. "I
had always been curious about the company, so one Thursday afternoon, I walked into their offices and asked the re-
ceptionist, who turned out to be the daughter of the
company president, for whatever literature they had about
the company," Rogers recalls. " 'Why don't you speak to
my father?' she said. I did, and in the course of that thirty-
minute conversation bells and whistles started to go off in
my head. I thought this was a rapidly growing company in
an interesting field. And I blurted out, 'Would you like to
sell your company?' "

Rogers didn't have any great insight that would lead him
to change the company, which in 1976 was doing about $6

million in sales a year and netting $250,000 on the two mil-
lion gallons of ice cream it sold. Quite the contrary. All he
wanted to do was see if Dreyer's could sell more ice cream.

Rogers reasoned that if you could take Dreyer's concept
of making the best ice cream possible—no matter what the
cost—beyond its northern California base, you'd be able to
take advantage of economies of scale and make money. Of
course by sticking to an all-premium product—and charging correspondingly high prices—you'd never get the domi-
nant share of the $3.5 billion ice cream market. After all,
not many people are going to pay $4.19 for a half-gallon of
rocky road when they can get Rocky Road that is almost as
good for $2.59. Still, you would do well enough.

Rogers's timing was perfect. As a curious offshoot of the
recession in the early 1980s, sales of gourmet products—
roughly defined as uncommon, high-cost, high-quality
items—had started to take off. People who couldn't afford
to go out to eat in restaurants were staying home, but making more elaborate dinners. Those stay-at-homes, coupled
with members of the World War II baby boom who liked
good, wholesome food and were willing to pay for it no
matter what the cost, started a surge in premium products.
Although overall food consumption only grows as fast as
America's waistline—about 1 percent a year—gourmet
products are expected to grow at about 3 percent through
at least 1990. Premium ice cream (such as Dreyer's) and
superpremiums (such as Haagen-Dazs) are growing even
faster. They now account for about 30 percent of ice cream
sales nationwide.

Rogers's unhappiness with the restaurant business, curiosity about the ice cream shop near his home, and
America's changing eating habits led to the creation in
1977 of Dreyer's Grand Ice Cream Inc. Dreyer's ice cream is
now a fixture in supermarkets west of the Mississippi. Sales
are growing 40 percent a year.

"The key to our success is that the company has never

compromised on the formulation and the ingredients in our ice cream. And there are so many ways to cheat," Rogers says almost wistfully. "The most extreme example is probably vanilla. Pure vanilla extract has cost as much as $140 a gallon. The vanilla substitute, which has a very similar taste, goes for something like a dime a gallon. Well, we use millions of dollars' worth of pure vanilla extract each year, and it would be easy to put those millions on the bottom line."

But Rogers—a man smart enough to look for one small opportunity in a field almost everyone else had written off—is not about to tamper with his formula for success. "Our goal is to be the premium ice cream company in this country."

## Why Aren't There More Entrepreneurs?

Lives there a red-blooded American old enough to work who has not had an idea for a new company? Who has not said on at least one occasion, "Someone could make a fortune if they'd just. . . ." So how come stories like Gary Rogers's are so rare?

Study the type of ideas on which highly successful growth companies were originally based, and you have to conclude that the reason there aren't more successful entrepreneurs is that there aren't many people with the need or nerve to try out their ideas. The successful entrepreneur is the person who makes an idea happen, even if there are a lot of unexpected problems and even if it's not a very good idea in the first place. That's one common thread you'll find.

Another, we are now convinced, is that most people approach the idea from the wrong premise. Rogers, and the others you will meet, didn't start with an original idea. They improved an existing one.

Unfortunately, when most people think about starting a

company, they envision a new concept. They plan to revolutionize the marketplace with a product that has never existed before. That thinking—while admirable—is wrong. Worse, it is unlikely to lead to the creation of a successful company. The reason becomes clear if you spend a couple of minutes trying to think of an item that doesn't exist now and bears no relationship to anything else in existence. You'll find it isn't easy.

Why is it so hard? It's not that there are no new things to be invented; there are. The problem is most of the underlying principles for any new product are already there. As soon as you say, "Someone should invent a software program that does . . ." you see the point. The program you are suggesting is new; the concept of software isn't.

---

*It doesn't have to be an original idea. Improving an existing one is quite adequate. And easier.*

---

But thinking of something unique is what most people start pondering when they begin looking for a product to launch them into business. That is exactly the wrong way to go. Instead of sulking about the fact that software has been invented, you should be grateful *you* don't have to invent it. That would be difficult. Your task is far easier. All you have to do is write a better program.

The problem with unique inventions, such as the Polaroid camera, lies in the uniqueness itself. Because the product is completely different, you spend a great deal of time—and money—educating your potential market about what you have and why they need it. Instead of filling an obvious need in the marketplace, you have to create the market for your product. Polaroid is an excellent example. While the idea of a camera that develops its own film eventually became a smash, it took an awfully long time to catch on. People had to learn what the camera did. And they had to be educated before Polaroid could ever hope to sell one camera.

Our favorite example of this is a terrific idea thought up by the people at Corning Glass: eyeglasses that change to sunglasses and back again depending on available light. The idea—as anyone who has ever lost a pair of prescription glasses can tell you—is wonderful: A lens that darkens when exposed to daylight and lightens as the daylight decreases means you don't need two pairs of prescription lenses.

So why are the vast majority of people who wear glasses—83 percent to be precise—still walking around with one pair of clear glasses and another pair of sunglasses, nineteen years after Corning began marketing its Photogray lenses?

Part of the reason, but only a minor part, is the reluctance of opticians to push the product. When an optician sells a plastic lens, he can tint it or etch it and thus charge more. Corning does not give him that chance. All the optician can do with a Corning lens is add a markup. Also, glass lenses are harder to work with than plastic ones. They take longer to grind. That's another reason for the optician's reluctance to tout the lens. And, of course, an optician can make more money selling two pairs of glasses—one clear, the other tinted—than he can just selling one frame with the Corning lenses.

But the easiest answer to why the photochromatic lenses haven't caught on is that people don't know about them.

"Surprisingly, after all the advertising we have done over the years, a lot of people don't know what photochromatic lenses are," says a somewhat sheepish corporate spokesman. "People don't grasp the notion that the eyeglasses change to a sunglass and back again. And that is the main message in our ads." A message that Corning has failed to get across, despite nineteen years of advertising.

The idea for a new product doesn't have to be original. If you want to increase your chances for success, it shouldn't be.

## The Entrepreneurial Copycat

It's one thing to say that an entrepreneurial idea doesn't have to be original. It is quite another to say that outright *copying* is entrepreneurial. But it can be. You can play Pepsi to Coca-Cola or Avis to Hertz. But there has to be a need in the marketplace.

Nine times out of ten that need is called monopoly. Break it, and you have filled a need: You have introduced competition.

While easy to say, that is far harder to do. You have to know the marketplace intimately to spot the opportunity. That's a key reason people who leave big companies to create their own business in a related field usually set up shop near their former employers. It keeps them close to the market they know best. That market is either one their former employer did not serve well, or a market searching for a second source of a material or service it needs. That alternative supplier is likely to be a copycat entrepreneur.

Here's the usual situation in which copying someone else's idea works: A company suddenly finds itself dependent on the supplier of one product or service. A computer company may be buying all its disk drives from a single manufacturer; an ice cream company might be getting all its milk from one dairy. The company becomes worried that its sole supplier might go out of business, be crippled by a strike, or start charging exorbitant rates. That concern creates an opportunity for an entrepreneur who can also provide the worried company with what it needs. All the entrepreneur has to do is offer the company a "me-too" product at a competitive rate. By breaking the monopoly of the first supplier, the entrepreneur creates an opportunity.

---

*It sounds strange, but copying an existing idea can be entrepreneurial.*

---

Copying also works where the market is so big and the product so basic that there is plenty of room for more than one supplier. Soft drinks, car rentals, and gasoline stations are simple examples of fields that are so large they can accommodate several companies that do virtually the same thing. But since there are only a finite number of huge markets, most of the copying occurs in smaller fields in which there are single-source suppliers. We will discuss two companies that are classic examples of this "me-too" approach to entrepreneurship in the "Marketing" section.

## Unique Is Not Better

David Mintz didn't engage in the process of me-tooism. For a long time, he probably wished he had. His story, when contrasted with Gary Rogers's of Dreyer's Grand Ice Cream, is perhaps the best example of why an original idea is the most difficult to make work.

Mintz was a successful New York restaurateur who specialized in catering Jewish celebrations—weddings and bar and bas mitzvahs. Jewish dietary laws forbid the eating of meat and dairy at the same meal, and that posed a problem for Mintz. Ice cream was one of the desserts he wanted to offer, but he couldn't if meat had been served during the meal.

What was needed, thought Mintz, was a dessert that tasted like ice cream but was not dairy-based. About nine years ago, he stumbled on the idea of using tofu, soybean curd, as his base.

The concept was simple, just as Gary Rogers's concept of deciding to produce only the best ice cream at Dreyer's was simple. But while both Rogers and Mintz are in the business of selling frozen desserts, that's where the similarities end.

At Dreyer's, Rogers's blueprint was easy to follow: Just use the best ingredients possible. Real vanilla, as opposed to chemical substitutes, for example. For Mintz it was anything but simple. "We went through countless formulas over the years to come up with a good-tasting ice cream substitute," he recalls.

And where Rogers found the concept of "premium" ice cream virtually self-explanatory, Mintz—who had come up with a unique idea—had to spend a lot of time just trying to get people to sample his product.

At first, Mintz asked people at his restaurant if they wanted to taste a tofu-based dessert. Mintz says he quickly stopped asking. "They got turned off as soon as I told them it had tofu in it."

While virtually tasteless, tofu's crumbly texture reminds many people of eating the paste they used during arts and crafts in kindergarten. So Mintz took another route. "I'd say, 'Try this new dessert.' They did, and they thought it was delicious." But Mintz had to keep repeating the education process each time he offered his confection, and once people heard there was tofu in it, their smiles faded. Lips puckered and orders stopped. Says Mintz: "At the beginning, we found no acceptance."

To overcome the reluctance, Mintz tried calling his product Ice Kream and playing up that it was a soybean product. Tofu appeared at the bottom of the label. "But as soon as they saw the word *tofu*, people were skeptical," Mintz recalls. "It turned them off. Would it have been easier if we had been trying to sell a premium ice cream? Sure."

Mintz eventually called his product Tofutti, and the cute name helped get people to try it. But more importantly, Mintz's concept finally caught up with the culture.

By the early 1980s, America's meat-and-potatoes diet was passé. It wasn't just "health nuts" who were eating better—everyone was, or wanted to. In their search for more nutrition people discovered Tofutti. They found it isn't fattening—about thirty-two calories an ounce, or about a third of that of a premium ice cream like Dreyer's—has no cholesterol or butterfat, and really does taste good. Mintz, who now heads the public company called Tofu Time, appears on his way to success.

Still, even given the change in America's eating habits, it took Mintz almost ten years to go from concept to profit because he had to constantly explain what he had. During those same ten years, Gary Rogers, with his instantly understandable product—a better-tasting ice cream—grew Dreyer's into a company with nearly $100 million in sales and net margins of 7 percent. Unique is not better.

Not only is unique not better, it is more difficult. To be able to create something that bears no relation to what now exists is an ability only very few people have. For the rest of us—indeed for every one of the entrepreneurs profiled in this book—the secret to creating a new company is making improvements in, or variations on, existing ideas.

Entrepreneurs don't wait until they have an original idea or (as we will see) even an important one; they go ahead with what they have or know.

# 3

## The Need (or Nerve) to Make Ideas Work

Variations on a theme are easier to create than the theme itself, as we saw in chapter 2. But what makes an entrepreneur go out and create those variations? Consider these three entrepreneurs:

- Bernard A. Goldhirsh started a sailing magazine because he thought the existing ones were too snooty. "They were all filled with Somebody the Third meeting up with Somebody Else the Fourth, at some fancy yacht club."

   But in the process of creating *Sail* magazine, Goldhirsh realized he knew nothing about starting or building a business. He learned everything by trial and error. In talking to friends about his problems, Goldhirsh learned other fledgling entrepreneurs were in the same boat.

   The result of that insight was *Inc.* magazine, devoted to small businesses and their concerns. It is one of the most successful start-ups in magazine history.

- Arthur A. Jones always had a secret obsession. The son of two doctors, Jones never made it to high school. "I dropped out in eighth grade. I should have done it in sixth."

He worked as everything from an animal importer to television producer, and even hosted the syndicated show "Wild Cargo." But through it all he kept a secret. Jones was fascinated with bodybuilding. Through conventional weightlifting techniques he had created an impressive physique, "but I wasn't satisfied."

For twenty-two years, more than eight thousand days, Jones used his spare time to try to develop a better means of bodybuilding. The result? The Nautilus machine and a small fortune.

- Perry Mendel was a successful real estate developer in the South. His kids were grown, and so there was no reason for him to be overly interested in child care back in 1968. Yet almost every day there was a "tremendous amount in the media about women entering the labor force. Women's liberation was in full swing. There were always stories about how hard it was to get domestic help and how inflation was forcing both husband and wife to work. Divorce was increasing. I got to wondering, 'Who was taking care of the children?' "

The answer, soon, would be Perry Mendel. In 1968, at the age of forty-six, he started Kinder-Care Learning Centers, now the largest professional operator of private day-care centers in the United States.


Goldhirsh, Jones, and Mendel are representatives of the people who started the best small companies in America. In each you find a strong desire to create something they thought was needed. Goldhirsh wanted to find a way to help people like himself learn more about business. Jones was searching for a more efficient bodybuilding technique, and Mendel was looking for a better form of child care. And although they never met Jack Massey, each was to fol-

low his prescription for wealth: They established a goal and
set out to accomplish it.

---

*Give the market what it needs—if it meshes with your
personal strengths and beliefs.*

---

What motivates different people is as different as the
people themselves. What motivates entrepreneurs boils
down to this: need or nerve—or both. People like Goldhirsh, Jones, and Mendel spot something that someone
truly needs and set out to create it. Or they are so unhappy
with their current lot that they chuck it all to do something
else. Necessity—for them—really is the mother of invention. If you are motivated enough, any idea can put you
into a new business, as we will see as we take a closer look at
these three men.


## "They Were Not Talking to Me"

How Bernie Goldhirsh became the multimillionaire publisher of an extremely successful magazine is a study in ser-
endipity—and intelligence.

The story begins right after Goldhirsh graduated high
school. A New York native, Goldhirsh grew up in Brooklyn
and Long Island and was admitted to M.I.T. While that
was a traditional route for a boy who was smart and loved
math, what happened once he got to school in Cambridge,
Massachusetts, was anything but traditional.

The problem surfaced right away. Goldhirsh's goals and
M.I.T.'s were incompatible. "At M.I.T., at the undergradu-
ate level, they give you problems to solve," he says. "That's
what they want you to do. The fun for me has always been
in creating those problems." The conflict led to Goldhirsh
dropping out. He returned a number of times to give college another try, but always would leave soon after.

Every time he dropped out, Goldhirsh took a different job. Sometimes he went to the Caribbean, signing on to crew on a sailing ship, to sate his love of the sea. Other jobs were more traditional, and it was during a stint as the head of the science department at a Cambridge prep school that Goldhirsh stumbled onto the road that would make him rich.

He loved teaching. Capturing ideas and explaining them was seductive. He also loved sailing. Why not create an onboard school where students could come for the summer to sail and to see the people they would otherwise meet only in textbooks?

Intellectually, the idea was a smash. Students and teachers loved it. Financially, it bombed. After a summer aboard his ninety-eight-foot ketch, Goldhirsh returned to Cambridge broke and searching for an idea that would generate enough money so he could spend all of his time working on the school.

Upon returning to Cambridge, Goldhirsh started giving courses in celestial navigation, which combined his love of math—steering by the stars is really just applied geometry—teaching, and sailing. "One day after class, a woman came up to me and said since the text I had written for the course was self-explanatory, I should think about running the school as a correspondence course," Goldhirsh recalls. And that's what he did. "It's a funny thing; in a correspondence course the students become your pen pals," he says. "They write you long letters about their interests, and you end up writing long letters back."

In those letters, Goldhirsh's students asked questions. More often than not they were concerned with practical sailing matters. "I have a family of four; what kind of boat should I buy?" and "How do I keep my two-year-old from falling overboard?" were typical.

It was clear that sailors, and would-be sailors, wanted two kinds of information that were hard to come by. They wanted to know what kind of boats would meet their needs. And they also needed practical sailing advice. Providing this information, Goldhirsh thought, might be the way of raising money for his school.

So Goldhirsh began writing small black-and-white booklets on practical aspects of sailing. He also wrote to sailboat manufacturers to see if they would advertise in a directory that listed technical specifications of every available sailboat. Recalls Goldhirsh: "All the advertising back then had pretty women in bathing suits and said, 'Our boats are the best and safest.' It is hard from that kind of ad to figure what to buy."

With a commitment from the boat manufacturers to advertise, Goldhirsh went searching for a printer. "I was honest about it. I told them I had no idea if I would be able to pay, since I didn't know if the directory would sell. So I offered a deal. If a printer was willing to assume the risk of not being paid, I would pay one-and-a-half times the going rate for the job if I made money."

The directory made money. That came as a surprise. And the heavy response from the small ads in the directory for Goldhirsh's sailing booklets came as an even bigger shock. "People started telling me that I should turn all those booklets into a magazine," Goldhirsh says.

There were, of course, sailing magazines already on the market. The biggest was *Yachting*. "But that was written for people who had grown up at their father's yacht club," Goldhirsh says. "There really was nothing for people who just wanted to learn about sailing."

And more people wanted to learn. Sailing was becoming popular in the late 1960s. The middle class was beginning to sail. They were buying boats, not yachts, for day trips or weekend jaunts, and wanted to know about their new hobby. To satisfy that curiosity, Goldhirsh officially ended his days as a self-professed boat bum and with sixty-five dollars in the bank started *Sail* magazine. Founded in 1970, the magazine turned profitable in 1972 and quickly became bigger than *Yachting*.

Goldhirsh was pleased, rich (he would sell the magazine to Meredith Corp., an Iowa-based media company, for more than $12 million), but not fulfilled.

His restlessness started while he was creating *Sail*. Eager to learn how to build a company, Goldhirsh turned to the business magazines. "I read *Forbes, Fortune, Dun's,* and really studied them. And it became clear they were not talking to me. They had a different reader in mind.

"I thought there should be a magazine for guys like me who were building little companies. I talked to my friends, and they said the same thing: The big business magazines were not all that relevant. I envisioned a magazine for people on that rocky voyage from the garage to the fully managed stage." That vision would become *Inc.* magazine.

Goldhirsh had started *Sail* to fill the needs of people not being served by existing publications. He started *Inc.* for exactly the same reason.

For example, in 1979 when the first issue of *Inc.* appeared, it took sales of $275 million to be included in the *Forbes* 500, a directory of the nation's five hundred largest companies. The focus on big companies had served publisher Malcolm Forbes extremely well (his net worth was recently estimated at more than $200 million). But the decision of *Forbes, Fortune,* and *Business Week* to concentrate on big companies meant that small companies, and the needs of people such as Goldhirsh and his friends were being ignored.

*Inc.*, which filled that void, was virtually an overnight success. Circulation climbed to 500,000 within five years and is now over 600,000 (*Business Week*'s circulation is about 860,000; *Forbes*'s, 725,000; and *Fortune*'s, about

710,000). "I knew *Inc.* would work; it was right," Goldhirsh says. "There was a need."

## "Faster Planes, Younger Women, Bigger Crocodiles"

"You don't do things because the world needs you to; you do things for your own purposes. People think that kind of motivation is evil. It's not."

So says Arthur A. Jones. His motivation for creating the Nautilus machine had little to do with benefiting mankind. In fact, Jones has a rather low opinion of mankind. ("If I ever met a man who thought, I'd kill him. He would be too dangerous to let live.") Jones was trying to solve a problem that had bothered him since childhood: How do you create a more efficient system of bodybuilding?

While outspoken on just about every topic from traditional forms of exercise ("worthless") to the meaning of life ("There are only three worthwhile things in this world: Younger women, faster airplanes, and bigger crocodiles"), Jones, sixtyish, professes not to know what attracted him to bodybuilding. He says it wasn't to show off. "I didn't go around flexing my muscles on streetcorners." Nor was it to get back at a bully who might have kicked dust in his face when he was growing up in Oklahoma. Nobody, says Jones, ever picked on him. "People instinctively know not to mess with me. I am not a violent person, but if you mess with me, you're in big trouble."

"I gave up trying to figure out my motivation a long time ago," Jones says. But there he was working out with barbells in a YMCA in Tulsa in 1948 and not happy with the results. "Other people might have been impressed, but I wasn't," he says gruffly. Jones tried longer workouts, shorter workouts, doing exercises in different combinations, but nothing worked. "I eventually realized the problem was not me, nor the exercises I was doing. It was the tool, the barbell."

The problem with barbells and other conventional exercises, Jones would conclude, is they don't make allowances for the human physique. At different points in an exercise, say, bench pressing (lifting a barbell from your chest over your head), people have differing degrees of strength.

As you lift the bar off your chest, you are fairly strong. But about halfway through the movement, lifting becomes difficult. If you can get past that point, the lift becomes easy again. But the barbell makes no allowances for how difficult, or easy, it is to go through the different parts of the lift. As a result, the amount of weight you can lift is limited by a muscle's weakest point.

What Jones started trying to create in 1948 was a "thinking man's barbell," one that would test a whole muscle through an exercise. It would decrease the resistance at the muscle's weakest point and increase it where the muscle was stronger. The solution, after numerous prototypes ("It would take ninety days to tell you about all the mistakes I made") is a cam and a series of weights. As the weights are lifted, the cam varies the resistance depending on the muscle's strength during the exercise. The cam looks like the shell of a nautilus mollusk, and gave Jones the company's name. America's concern about its growing waistline gave him his success.

As people became more conscious of keeping fit in the 1970s, the search was on for less boring forms of effective exercise. If not the Holy Grail, Nautilus would do. A workout on a series of eight Nautilus machines takes about eighteen minutes and only needs to be repeated three or four times a week. Suddenly, bodybuilding—which used to be done only by men in gyms that always seemed to smell of stale sweat socks—became a coed activity. Gyms turned into "health clubs," invariably featuring Nautilus equipment, and became the singles' bars of the 1980s.

But during the twenty-two years Jones worked to create the Nautilus machine, he was not thinking about changing the ways that many Americans exercise or court. He says he never even thought about the commercial possibilities of his creation. "I did it because I was curious. Having the money is okay, but I had been rich before. [In his animal importing/television days.] I wanted to see if I could create a more efficient form of exercise. When I am presented with a problem, I don't rest until I solve it.

"Achievement comes from reaching your goals," Jones says. "I own three 707s now, and I want 747s. When I get them, I will probably want a Concorde, and after that a B-1 bomber. Anyone who has achieved their goals has set them too low."

## "Somebody Has to Take Care of the Children"

The idea that would lead to the creation of the nation's largest chain of child-care centers did not come from divine inspiration, exhaustive research, or even luck. Perry Mendel read about it in a newspaper.

The papers in 1968 were filled with news of women entering the work force in record numbers and how the soaring divorce rate was increasing the number of single-parent homes. Mendel, a successful real estate developer who built homes and shopping centers in his native South, got to wondering about who would be taking care of the children once all those women went back to work.

Why was he thinking about such things? After all, his own kids were long since grown. "I think it was the entrepreneurial spirit," Mendel says. "I wasn't bored with what I was doing. I just kept seeing all those stories and thought, boy, what a terrific idea for franchising. There clearly was a need that wasn't being met.

"But the clincher was that in the now-defunct *National Observer* there was a big headline about Performance Systems Inc., which ran the Minnie Pearl restaurants, and how they were going to start a chain of child-care centers," Mendel recalls. "The *pro forma* figures they gave looked so fantastic that it really got me motivated. So I worked up my own figures, put together a group of investors, and we started out with two hundred thousand dollars."

The key to success, Mendel quickly realized, was in eliminating the guilt parents felt in leaving their children in a day-care center. After all, those early members of the baby boom, who were now having children of their own, had grown up having a mother who was waiting in the kitchen with milk and cookies when they came home from school. That was the childhood they knew. Even the television shows they were raised on, "Father Knows Best," "Ozzie and Harriet," and the like never pictured a mother working anyplace other than around the house. But now it was not uncommon for both parents to work. And many of them worried they were depriving their children of a "normal" upbringing by putting them in a day-care center.

---

*People feel guilty about many things they have little control over. Figure out a way to eliminate that guilt, and they will pay you well.*

---

"I figured if we could take away the guilt, we would be a success," Mendel recalls. "The way to do that was to offer the working parent something her children couldn't get if they were left with grandma or the woman down the street who was taking care of three or four children to make ends meet."

That something was a day-care center structured along the lines of a nursery school. Some of the staff would be trained in early childhood development. "In addition to letting the children play, they would be teaching them social amenities—how to share and so forth," Mendel says. Instead of feeling guilty about leaving their children, parents would feel they were helping their child learn.

The concept, as Kinder-Care's success (it now has well over one thousand centers, and Mendel is projecting 30 percent sales and earnings growth through 1990) shows, was a hit. But it didn't happen overnight. True to his initial vision, Mendel started Kinder-Care as a franchise operation. It was the wrong way to go.

---

*If your market requires you to change your original concept, change it. It does no good to lose money while sticking to the "perfect" idea.*

---

"Our program was structured like McDonald's. We offered financing help, site selection, etc.," Mendel says. "We went through some tight money times when it became very difficult to arrange for the tons of dollars we needed. Plus the people we were dealing with were not business persons. The problem with franchising to the people who were attracted to the business—the ex-schoolteacher and the like—was that while they loved children, they knew nothing about real estate and nothing about financing. They needed Kinder-Care to do it all. If we were going to do it all, we needed to own it all. Our franchise fee just wouldn't cover costs."

But even when Mendel stopped franchising ("the smartest corporate decision we ever made") seven months after he began, there still was a major hurdle: the newness of the concept itself. Up until Kinder-Care, there wasn't large-scale day-care. Despite its grand plans, Performance Systems—the company that had inspired Mendel when he read about it in the paper—wasn't successful.

Mendel found it hard to convince parents to bring their children to his centers. "We went through some very rough times early in our corporate life," he recalls in his office in Montgomery, Alabama. "At all times our schools produced profits, but our overhead was very high because of all the people necessary to make sure our schools produced the quality we required. We did not have enough schools to amortize those costs.

"In the summer of 1970, [about a year after Kinder-Care opened] we had seventeen schools, and we were at wit's end. Our coffers were just about depleted. I remember going to lunch with my executive vice-president, Richard Grassgreen, and saying, 'Richard, I don't know if we are going to make it with these seventeen schools. Financing is tough and money is very tight. If enrollment isn't up by September, I guess you'll go back to practicing law, and I will run the seventeen schools.' That is how close we came to being a very small outfit."

What happened, of course, is Mendel made his quota and stayed open, although he would merge with Warner National Corp. to gain the financing necessary to expand. Mendel bought his company back six years later and has been successful ever since.

"Our concept made sense," Mendel says in describing his success. "Right now a little more than half of all women work. In the 1990s, two out of every three females will be in the labor force. Somebody has to take care of their children. And over the long run, our centers make sense for the children, too. Sooner or later children must be with their peers.

"I have not been surprised about how well we have done. My philosophy is that if there is a need, and you can develop a product or a service to satisfy that need, there is no reason you should not be successful."

## What They All Had in Common

Mendel, Jones, and Goldhirsh each had a vision. None of them involved radically new thinking. Mendel got a rough draft of his business plan from a newspaper article. Barbells were more than 100 years old before Jones began tinkering with what would become the Nautilus machine, and specialty magazines, like Goldhirsh's *Inc.*, have existed since Gutenberg. What these three men did was apply their knowledge to an existing product and make it better. That is typical of the successful entrepreneur. Henry Ford did not invent the automobile, and there were hamburger stands long before Ray Kroc took the McDonald brothers' idea beyond California.

But in addition to their ability of improving an existing idea, Mendel, Jones, and Goldhirsh had the need and nerve necessary to turn their vision into reality.

*Need* is the only word that can explain why Jones would spend twenty-two years working to develop the prototype of the Nautilus machine. And would anyone without Bernie Goldhirsh's nerve be willing to take the $12 million he received for selling *Sail* and gamble it on *Inc.*'s success? If someone handed you a check for $12 million, would you rush out and start another business? Especially one the experts said was destined to fail?

"I remember discussing my idea for starting *Inc.* with a friend who worked for McGraw-Hill [publishers of *Business Week* and other magazines]. He said I should talk it over with friends of his, three senior executives who had just retired.

"So I met with the three wise men, and to a man, they told me *Inc.* would never work. There was no need. People who were running small businesses were being adequately served by the existing publications. But they didn't understand what I was telling them."

They couldn't see Bernie Goldhirsh's vision. Nor could they know of the need and nerve he had to turn that vision into reality.

# 4

## How to Spot an Opportunity

While no one can teach you how to spot an opportunity—
you'll either recognize it, or you won't—there are some
simple tests you can apply in order to increase your chances
of successfully building a company. The best place to apply
these tests is in areas that *you* understand. While you can
change fields to create a new product, you increase your
chances of success by sticking closer to home, since you
won't have to waste time learning the basics of your business. It takes a lot longer to come up with the perfect choco-
late chip cookie recipe if you have never been in a kitchen.

---

*Ask yourself how you can compete differently, either by
upgrading, downgrading, bundling, unbundling, transporting an idea to another area, going mass-market, spe-
cializing, or competing on price.*

---

All of the following tests involve spotting a niche and
filling it. Now niche seeking and niche filling are things
consultants and professors always tell entrepreneurs to do.
But they never quite define what they mean. It has become
a buzzword with no meaning behind the buzz.

Niche filling boils down to this: Competing Differently.
If an entrepreneur looks at the marketplace and sees a small
void he can fill, he has spotted a niche. But what he really has

done is looked at the way others are competing and concluded he can be successful if he does things differently.

Consider regional airlines. Following deregulation in the 1970s, major carriers like TWA and United stopped serving smaller cities. It wasn't economical to fly big planes to places where they would arrive and depart predominantly empty. That left a hole, or niche, in the marketplace that airlines—ranging in size from Piedmont and Ozark to Mississippi Valley and Precision—rushed to fill.

You could describe what those regional airlines did as niche filling. But you would paint a more accurate picture if you said, Following airline deregulation, companies such as Precision Airlines noticed its larger competitors had abandoned flying to and from smaller cities in New England. The bigger airlines had also stopped linking Boston and New York with those small towns. So Precision began flying between places like Springfield, Vermont, and Keene, New Hampshire, and made sure it had flights to and from those towns and Boston. In other words, Precision found a different way of competing within the airline market.

All entrepreneurs search for ways of competing differently. Here are strategies they follow.

## Ten Ways Of Competing Differently

1. *Upgrade.* Take a basic product and make it special, either by adding value to it or marketing it as a status product. Luxury automobiles, designer blue jeans, or gourmet cookies are examples of what were once pedestrian products that have been given cachet.

In each case, the underlying concept remains unchanged. Just the product's image has been improved. It is no longer merely a car, but a status symbol. Basic jeans are now a fashion item, and cookies, once a simple, inexpensive treat, have become something worthy of an epicure.

But all that has really changed is the perception of the

product. A luxury car is still something that takes you from here to there. Designer jeans remain pants, and gourmet cookies still taste good with milk. It is the image of these products that has been altered dramatically—along with their price tag.

**2.** *Downgrade.* Take a product that has always been associated with status and reduce it to its underlying concept.

Examples: People Express Airlines eliminated all the frills that came with an airplane ticket (meals, magazines, etc.) and reduced flight to simple transportation. The Wright brothers didn't show movies aboard when they took off from Kitty Hawk, and neither does People Express. Rent-a-Wreck car rentals, which loans you a beat-up heap at a discount instead of a shiny new car, is a similar idea. And if you look on the supermarket shelves you now see everything from generic beer to no-name cooking oil competing against Budweiser and Crisco.

**3.** *Bundle.* There are certain products or services that almost always go together. Instead of requiring people to pay for them separately, combine them. A good example is the Adam computer made by Coleco. Most computer manufacturers, such as IBM and Apple, require you to purchase separately the hardware (computer, printer, etc.) and the software (word processing programs, spreadsheets, and the like) necessary to make a computer work.

While not as powerful a machine as the IBM or Apple, Adam combined everything in one unit. The problems Coleco had selling the Adam stemmed from the quality and reliability of the components used—not the concept. People loved the idea; they just hated Coleco's execution. Coleco abandoned Adam in early 1985. There is good reason to think that if another company tried the idea, it would work.

Another good example of bundling is an idea that

seems to be catching on now: popular priced restaurants that show current movies during your meal. Instead of going out for a hamburger before or after the picture show, the two are combined. (We had always thought that drive-in movies served a similar function in courtship—entertainment and privacy—but a few people say they have gone to drive-ins and actually watched an entire movie.)

**4.** *Unbundle.* Just the flip side of what we discussed above. Ask, What products have been so gussied up that you can sell the individual components? Life insurance is a good example. It became common practice in the industry to combine the protection component with a savings element. That became the basic insurance policy. Term insurance, which eliminates the savings component and just provides protection, has become very popular.

Other examples of unbundling range from the obvious to the subtle. For example, selling sports jackets might not qualify as unbundling (a person doesn't always need another pair of pants), but *People* magazine clearly does. A popular way of reading *Time* magazine has always been starting at the back, where the "soft" features like the "People" section are. *Time* spun off that highly read section and made it a separate magazine.

Spin-offs occur all the time in television. Popular characters in one series are given a show of their own. The Jeffersons, who were Archie Bunker's neighbors in "All in the Family," moved to their own show. "Trapper John, M.D." was spun off from "M*A*S*H," a television series that itself had been adapted from the Robert Altman movie, which had been based on a book. You get the idea.

Less obvious is breaking a product down into its separate components and then selling each component separately. Consider any high-tech product. If you were to divide it into two separate parts, you could say there is the technology itself and the manufacturing process. Suppose instead of combining the two components to produce a product, you just stopped at step one, the technology. You could take the technology and license it. That would be an example of unbundling.

Similarly, every business is composed of people with specialized skills performing tasks that make their company unique. Suppose we separated the people from the business and had them perform those tasks for someone else. They would, in essence, become consultants, and they would be another example of unbundling.

**5.** *Transport.*   If a product sells in one area, take it to another. If you stop and think about it, that is what importing and exporting are all about. But you can go beyond just selling white wine from France in New Jersey, or opening a Chinese restaurant in Kansas City.

For example, Europe and California—for whatever reasons—tend to create new products and ideas ahead of the rest of the world. How about someone from Massachusetts taking a drive up and down the coast of California looking for new ideas in fast food, entertainment, whatever? Once you find what is working in Modesto, why not try it back home in Marblehead?

One potential problem with transporting an idea is that you may need more than just the idea to make it work. Let's take an easy example. Was the secret of McDonald's the fact that they sold hamburgers of consistent quality quickly? Probably not. In addition to the hamburgers that always tasted the same, the company offered friendly service in bright and cheerful restaurants that were always clean. Without each component, it is unlikely the company would have done as well. After all, no matter how dependable the food, if the restaurant and rest rooms aren't clean, the customer is less likely to go back.

To reduce the number of things that can go wrong in transporting an idea, ask for a franchise on the concept you like. That way you reduce the variables involved. Also, look for places where existing ideas have not yet reached. While it seems every hamlet has a hamburger stand, in the 1970s CPT, a Minnesota word processing company, found that IBM and Wang, the leaders in word processing, had virtually ignored selling in smaller cities and towns. So that is where CPT concentrated its efforts and did well. Wal-Mart used the same strategy in bringing big department stores to Smalltown, U.S.A., and in the process made founder Sam Walton one of America's richest men.

You don't have to stop at the borders of the continental United States. Ask, What items, or trends, are now popular in Europe? Would they work here? In what areas does the rest of the world lag behind the United States? What is working here that I can set up there? As the people who run Disneyland found, Mickey Mouse and friends have universal appeal. You can now find Disney theme parks in Japan and France. That idea was transported overseas. Conversely, you can find Americans munching on croissants and drinking sake here.

**6.** *Mass-market.*    Take an idea that has been very successful in one narrow area and see if it will work on a broader scale. This is what Gary Rogers decided to do in expanding Dreyer's Grand Ice Cream beyond its northern California base. It is what every company does when it takes a product "national."

It is also the underlying concept behind the "buy and build" strategy now being employed successfully by several large companies. Instead of creating new products and introducing them nationwide, companies—especially those in food and packaged goods—are searching out regional products such as Thomas's English Muffins and Entenmann's desserts. Big companies such as The Sara Lee Corp. and General Foods buy these regional favorites and then introduce them to the rest of the country. As long as the acquisition costs are less than building a winner from scratch—and they usually are since about 80 percent of all new products fail—it is a very·profitable strategy.

Pillsbury is one company that has done this particularly well. It has acquired restaurant chains as diverse as Burger King and Godfather's Pizza to successfully supplement its slow-growing consumer food business. Pillsbury now trails only McDonald's as the nation's leading restaurant company.

A variation on this is taking a product that has been used in a very specific way and trying to find a larger audience for it. Alan J. Zakon, chairman of the Boston Consulting Group, is a man who has given the idea of competing differently a great deal of thought. Lestoil is a favorite mass-marketing example of his. Originally designed as an industrial cleaner, it found acceptance when it was labeled a consumer product and introduced into the kitchens and bathrooms of America.

**7.** *Narrowcast.* We borrow the term from television. When cable television was in its infancy its broadcasters realized they all shouldn't try to reach mass audiences. For all their faults, the three networks do a fairly good job of serving the widest audience possible (even if they do occasionally offer shows like "Me and the Chimp").

The solution for cable operators was to narrowcast, or gear shows on a given channel to a particular audience. And so you have channels that show nothing but sports or movies or rock videos. There is even an all-weather station.

If you are up against a wide number of competitors in your field, and the potential audience is huge, you might be better off aiming for one specific segment instead of trying to reach everyone.

**8.** *Think big.* Instead of carrying just one product, carry everything related to it. Consumer electronics is one business in which that strategy has worked particularly well. Instead of opening a store that just sells stereo equipment, these retailers have added television sets, projection TVs, VCRs, computers, and every other consumer electronic gizmo there is. Customers walk into a store like Circuit City, Federated, or Highland and say, "Gosh, if they don't have it, I probably don't need it," and often walk out carrying a sales slip.

**9.** *Think small.* While huge stores—such as the ones run by the consumer electronics giants—can offer more merchandise, they can't offer the depth of selection in each line that a true connoisseur demands. Also, they usually don't have a trained staff on hand to offer advice.

You can succeed by offering more in a smaller field. For example, scores of stereo shops still succeed because they know not everyone wants the preamp and the amplifier built into the receiver. These smaller stores, which stick just to stereo, offer the units separately and provide the service a big store simply can't.

**10.** *Price.* On first blush, you may not think of competing on price as niche finding, but it is. Remember, we are talking about competing differently, and price is clearly one way to differentiate you from your competitors.

There are four ways you can compete on price. You can offer more value—real or perceived—at a higher price. If everyone is selling blue jeans for eighteen dollars a pair, and you make yours fit more snugly around the seat and charge twenty-five dollars, you are offering more (perceived?) value at a higher price.

Similarly, if a "regular" half-gallon of ice cream costs $2.89, and you use only premium ingredients and charge $4.19, you are again offering more value at a higher price.

The additional value offered doesn't have to be tangible. For example, the way that local suburban stores have sur-

vived the advent of shopping malls is by providing convenience and service. The hometown store is, by definition,
closer than the shopping mall, and if the sales help is
friendly and more attentive, you may be reluctant to trun-
dle off to the mall, where prices are better but service worse.

The second way to compete on price is to offer more
value for the same money. Your competitors are offering a
gallon of perfectly good paint at $10.99. If you sell a
longer-lasting, better-quality paint at the same price, you
are offering more value for the same money.

Third, you can offer the same value at a lower price. Everyone sells tea kettles for $3.98. If you can sell the same-
quality kettle for $3.49, you are offering the same value at a
lower price. (Just make sure you can make money doing it.)

Finally, you can offer less quality at a far lower price.
The competition sells tires that last fifty thousand miles for
a hundred dollars apiece. You sell a tire that will last only
twenty-five thousand miles, 50 percent as long, for forty
dollars, or 60 percent cheaper. You are offering less value at
a far lower price.

Not surprisingly, many of the strategies outlined here can
be combined. For example, you could create a large consumer electronics store (*Thinking big*) that sells only premium products (*Upgrade*) and sells them cheaper than
anyone else (*Price*).

---

*In asking how you can compete differently, don't limit
yourself to new ways of approaching the market. Sometimes, bringing back an old idea can work wonders.*

---

And while all the examples we used showed new ways of
approaching a market, that, of course, is not the only way
to compete differently. You could approach the market the

same way people did in Grandma's time. In other words, you can compete differently by offering things that nobody does any more.

Examples: house calls. Having the doctor come to you, as opposed to you schlepping to the doctor, is clearly an example of *upgrading;* you are adding value to a commodity. The commodity in this case is the doctor's visit. The value you have added is the convenience of the doctor coming to you.

Another idea worth reviving involves *narrowcasting.* Suppose you were to start a radio station that once again had dramas, mysteries, and comedies. You'd certainly be approaching the market differently. Given the diversity of the radio audience, it might work. After all, in recent years everything from the Big Band sound to Top 40 has made a comeback on radio.

The secret here is simply to ask, What is not being done any more? Once you come up with an idea, you have discovered a way to compete differently. Then the question becomes: Can you make the idea work economically?

The strategies we have outlined are examples of what other entrepreneurs have done to compete differently. One of the approaches, all of them, or some combination might be applicable to you. The best person to determine what will work in your specific field is you.

If you are thinking about going out on your own, we leave you with the best piece of advice we have ever read.

"You know more than you think you do."
                              Dr. Benjamin Spock,
                              *Baby and Child Care*

# 5

# What It Takes to Make Your Idea a Success

If you wait until you have a completely original idea or an "important" idea, you will wait forever. People like Rogers of Dreyer's Grand Ice Cream and Bernie Goldhirsh of *Inc.* didn't wait until they thought of something unique. Truly original ideas are hard to come by and, even worse, take a long time to explain to your potential market. In the years it took David Mintz to educate people about Tofutti, Rogers was building Dreyer's into a major ice cream company.

But while Mintz took the harder route in building a successful company, he did understand the most basic concept in creating an emerging growth company: Establish a commercial goal and then set off to accomplish it. None of these entrepreneurs—all of whom are now extremely wealthy— went into business to get rich. Rather, each looked at the market and then tried to fill a need, based on their own individual strengths.

Both components—the market's need and your ability to accomplish it—must be present if the idea is to work.

It wasn't enough that Perry Mendel was able to see the coming need for organized child care and felt compelled to try to meet it. What made the idea work was his understanding of real estate, which allowed him to arrange the financing and select the sites that would make Kinder-Care centers succeed. The market's need was there, but so was Mendel's ability to fill it. But again, Mendel's goal was not to become the multimillionaire he now is. His objective was creating a better way of taking care of the children of working parents.

Get-rich-quick schemes don't work. Think for a minute about the thousands of "entrepreneurs" who were going to make millions by selling computer software or renting movies for videocassette recorders. Very few of them ever made a dollar. They failed for the same reason get-rich-quick schemes always fail. These "entrepreneurs" plunged into the "hot" market, where, by definition, the competition is fiercest, and they weren't prepared.

Carried away with the thought of instantly becoming rich, they didn't take the time to study their competition or even determine what the market really wanted. To say, as people did a couple of years ago, "Everyone is going to need software. I'll open a store," is meaningless. What people? Personal computer users or businesses? What software? Programs for high-end personal computers, such as IBM and Apple, or for far cheaper computers which are basically game machines? The list of questions they didn't ask is endless. Should I discount? Sell by mail? Sell more than software? But perhaps the most basic question of all was: Do I understand this market? If I don't, should I believe the projections that computers will become as common as calculators?

Most of the people who owned the now-shuttered computer software stores never asked these questions. Their only goal was to make money. And without the discipline of establishing a commercial goal and then methodically setting off to accomplish it, that will never happen.

But if you are committed to filling a need in the market—and you have the nerve necessary to try out your idea—there is a major shortcut you can take. Look at what your competitors are doing and ask, What can I do differently? That is what is really meant when people say you should find a niche.

Is everyone selling a bundled product? Then maybe you can succeed by stripping it to its basics. It worked for People Express and Charles Schwab Discount Brokers. Have your competitors decided they are in a commodity business? Then maybe there is a place for taking that basic product and making it special. Look at how well Murjani did with Gloria Vanderbilt blue jeans.

None of these ideas required creating something unique. Airlines, stockbrokers, and blue jeans had been around forever. These entrepreneurs didn't wait for a divine revelation to put them in business, and neither should you.

Do wait until you have a firm grip on the marketing, financing, and production steps you will have to take simultaneously in order to launch your business. This is your business plan and what you'll need to raise seed money.

We will be discussing this planning process in detail in the next section. As you will see, your first planned steps, like your idea, don't have to be original. Just effective.

All this crucial homework takes a lot of time and effort. And most people with good ideas don't want to be bothered with homework. But you have to do it, and you have to do it before you get started. Once you are under way, you won't have time.

# Part II
# MARKETING

# 6

## A Word about Venture Capitalists

- Will a lot of people be willing to pay real money for this product or service?

- Enough money for this company to make enough money to grow on?

- What do we do if something goes wrong?

There's no ducking those. They're the obvious marketing questions every entrepreneur must ask himself at the outset.

Will there be enough people willing to spend their money to justify you spending yours? Do you have enough evidence to convince the venture capitalists? The bankers? While many entrepreneurs hate to admit it, moneymen often do have some pretty valuable experience to offer. They can spot some of the pitfalls you may encounter. They can tide you over the rough spots in the developmental phase. Also you can generally count on them to take you public at the best moment. And most important, they're there as devil's advocates when you're planning your next move.

That's why it's always a useful exercise to put your proposed corporate strategy at risk before these seasoned skeptics in the form of a business plan. You might not buy their conclusions. You may privately sneer at their apparent greed. You may bridle at their seemingly endless, doubting questions. But never forget that as an entrepreneur you're naturally biased toward optimism. A little tempering of that enthusiasm with the cold water of their bad experience could prove constructive. Very few businessmen—small, corporate, or entrepreneurial—have the crucial ability to assess coldly and disinterestedly their true strengths and weaknesses. So look upon venture capitalists as commercial psychiatrists of a sort.

What do venture capitalists look for in the business plan—a piece of paper that scarcely existed fifteen years ago?

Ted Schlissel, a C.P.A. who engineered the financial side of Reeves Telecommunication's initial success and has since advised dozens of other entrepreneurs says: "Today the business plan is the place where you demonstrate whether you really do or don't have a grasp of the business that you are a part of, whether you do or don't have a vision, whether you do or don't understand the economics of the business and the competition, and whether you do or don't understand the financing required while you are developing your product and struggling to find a place for it in the market. What venture capitalists look for is some assurance that the founder can think several moves ahead on every piece he has on the board as a chess player would ... in as realistic and perceptive a way as possible."

One business plan Schlissel helped write launched Data Switch very successfully in 1980. From the outset Schlissel was impressed by founder Richard Greene, an ex-IBM salesman. But he couldn't understand what Greene wanted to do at first. "It's a maxim in the venture capital business that if a man can't describe his business on the back of his business card he hasn't gotten to the core of what he's doing," says Schlissel. "It's like the guy who wrote his friend a ten-page letter. And his friend says, 'Why a ten-page letter? You could have written me a half a page.' The guy says, 'I didn't have the time.' "

Eventually Schlissel figured out how that half-page letter should read: "Here was a very slick guy with a great sales personality who wanted first to acquire the rights to distribute other people's products, trading on his sales prowess to generate funds. Only then would he start developing his own product, a data flow traffic cop for big computers. I thought that was a unique way to go at it."

Next question: What were the critical variables that would spell the difference between success and failure? Greene couldn't answer that. So Schlissel kept digging, often drawing diagrams to try to force Greene to abstract general principles from the specifics. "Finally I figured out that his business would be driven by the number of salespeople he had, at least in the beginning, and that we'd better know what it cost to train the right kind of salesman." In a fast-paced field like data processing, when you can introduce a new product is the most important question there is.

These were questions Greene hadn't asked himself. He was concentrating on his new product and what market niche it was aimed at.

---

*When you know you have a technological advantage in a high-tech business, get your product on the market at once. Don't wait until it's technically perfect.*

---

Schlissel's experience is by no means unique. Ask venture capitalists what they are looking for when they read a would-be entrepreneur's business plan, and they will answer: a document that just describes the opportunity. "The two things we're looking for are (1) is management backable? and (2) has the company met the test of the market-

place?" says Ed Glassmeyer, general partner of Oak Investment Partners and a veteran of Citicorp Venture Capital
and the venture capital arm of Wall Street's Donaldson
Lufkin & Jenrette. "That means the founders have to be
honest with themselves, as well as having the drive, determination, experience, and all that. Since by nature entrepreneurs are optimists, they often delude themselves. They
leave out the bad news. Or they don't really know their
product technically. One of the big mistakes we've made,
for example, is misjudging the amount of time it will take
to bring the product to market because there's a communi-
cations gap within the company. We want some evidence
that they are working off a plan."

Another thing the venture capitalist is NOT looking for
is surface perfection. "We're not searching for the beautifully prepared business plan," says Glassmeyer. "We'd
rather see somebody write out on the back of an envelope
what it is they think they really can do. We want management to stumble and fumble its way to a plan themselves.
That's a better test of their abilities than what some consultant can do for them. You can get a brilliantly con-
structed business plan that addresses the theoretical need.
Then you discover that the need has not been properly
identified, often because the entrepreneur is preoccupied
with a technical breakthrough. But he hasn't really figured
out a market for it. So you get a great business plan but a
lousy business.

"One reason why most successful entrepreneurs come out
of the same business that they're going into with their new
companies," Glassmeyer adds, "is that they can write a
good business plan because they really know the needs of
the marketplace."

Even successful entrepreneurs can make critical and re-
vealing mistakes in their business plans, says Glassmeyer.
That happened initially with Seagate, a manufacturer of

disk drives for microcomputers. "The first business plan said there's a need in the market for a smaller-diameter, high-capacity diskette, because there's going to be a greater generation of data at the small-business level, and you're going to need higher-capacity storage."

True enough, but Seagate's founders maintained that the market would pay a premium for its new products because they were smaller and more compact. Oak Investments took issue with that assumption. "We said we don't believe that," says Glassmeyer. "If the product is going to be smaller, it's going to be cheaper. So we sent the business plan back and told them if they could drive the cost down so they could price it more cheaply, then we'd be interested. Nine months later they did, and we financed the project." Seagate's subsequent success confirmed the venture capitalists' pricing judgment.

Why wouldn't executives experienced with that business come to that same conclusion themselves? They overestimated the time they had to exploit a technological advantage. "They thought they could drive the price down as they got volume up," Glassmeyer says. Oak Investments doubted Seagate would have as much time as they thought. Dealing as they do in a broad cross-section of businesses, venture capitalists can develop a keen, disinterested feeling for the pace of innovation in specific markets. "Product life cycles today are unbelievably short," says Glassmeyer. "So business planning is a very good way to protect yourself against underestimating the competition and overestimating the product life. In high-tech businesses today product lives are down around one year, when not too many years ago they were three to five years. What you're looking for, of course, is a narrow application—a niche."

If the life expectancy of a high-tech innovation is one year, that means an entrepreneur should start looking for his second and third new products the minute he sets up shop. It also suggests he should keep reformulating his business plan.

Glassmeyer puts it this way: "Resourcefulness is the critical quality you like to see in an entrepreneur. There are so many obstacles to winning. You can map out all the risks and alternatives in a business plan and still find yourself confronted with things you never anticipated. Obviously, the more diligent you are in the planning process the more likely you are to anticipate those obstacles."

For this reason venture capitalists like Glassmeyer try to maintain a continuing close rapport with management long after the initial investment. "The key to being a successful venture capitalist is to have management call you," he says. "You want them to feel so comfortable with you as a partner that they'll call up and say, 'Hey, I just want to share with you this concern I have.'"

The entrepreneur who can answer the tough questions an Oak Investment will raise about his business plan is also the entrepreneur who appreciates the fact that the questions were asked in the first place. He knows that he can't afford to surround himself with strong, experienced executives who would ask those same skeptical questions. He is also smart enough to recognize that the venture capitalist's skepticism is generally based on solid experience.

Generally speaking, the rule of thumb in venture capital investments is that one in ten succeed brilliantly, one or two others survive, and the rest fail. Those are long odds.

Let's go back to those original basic questions: Can you reasonably expect to generate enough profits from a big enough market to repay your backers and at the same time build a base for tomorrow?

Secondly, what is your fallback position? What are you going to do when the competition counterattacks? You know they will. What are you going to do about it?

While you ponder those questions don't worry about figuring out when to make your first public stock offering. Your venture capitalist backers will do that for you. After all, that's how they make their money. Going public is not a game for amateurs, even when Wall Street is in love with young start-up ventures.

Glassmeyer: "The question of when you should go public, or make your first public offering, doesn't tie necessarily to when you're profitable or when you've achieved a certain revenue level. What it ties more to are things like order backlog. You don't want to go public without any order backlog because you don't want to have your succeeding quarters turn out to be below the estimates made for the company. That means the company shouldn't go public until the product has been fully checked out and shipped and the company has happy customers. You don't have to be profitable, but your backlog has to be real."

---

*Don't worry about when to go public. Your venture capitalist knows more about it than you do, and timing your initial public offering correctly is how he makes his money.*

---

But the overriding consideration in the timing of an initial public offering is the stock market's mood. Again, the venture capitalist is much closer to the market than you are and therefore is better able to assess that mood. "The initial public offering market is very volatile, and there are different kinds of projects that appeal to the public at different times," says Glassmeyer. "Right now large discount retailing deals are very attractive. But they are in some sense the exception."

Not long ago, the market for initial public offering was weak. Just a few years ago, however, the stock market was ready to fall in love with almost any initial public offering. "In 1983 underwriters were looking for companies to take public," says Glassmeyer. "It's very hard to resist going public if someone says 'I've got $20 million for you, and you only have to give up 10 percent to 15 percent of the company.' So there were a number of premature public offerings—I think a lot of those companies would have rather worked their early mistakes through quietly than having to be out there with their board trying to explain them. Of course with that amount of capital you can usually cover a multitude of sins. So the bottom line is if the management team is in place, it really doesn't matter whether you're $5 million or $20 million in revenue. Then if you get a chance to go public you should go."

The problem arises when the entrepreneur's own skills are suited only to the early stages of a company's developments. A venture capitalist who backs him without realizing that is bound to run into trouble. Of course it is as difficult to spot such a limitation as it is to convince that entrepreneur that he should pass the baton to a successor for his own good. "That's one of the jobs of a venture capitalist," says Glassmeyer. "And that's another reason why these entrepreneurs don't love us. We try to sell them the idea of grooming a successor on the basis of their own investment in the company. Sometimes they'd be better off if the place were managed by someone who's had experience growing businesses."

Everyone knows the Over-The-Counter market has had more than its share of underwriters who exercised far less diligence than Glassmeyer describes. But such excesses, which the Securities and Exchange Commission cannot begin to police adequately, have attracted a more effective policeman of late: class-action lawyers looking for fraud or misleading statements in the prospectuses of initial public offerings. "The threat of litigation means that venture-backed companies are going to go public more carefully than they would have," says Glassmeyer. "It may pay you to wait another year or two before you go public."

Now let's get down to cases.

# 7

## To Catch a Surgeon

Let's start with the classic reason for starting your own company, an invention. In the following case it was someone else's invention that hadn't quite worked initially.

Back in 1964 Leon Hirsch was frustrated in the thin-margin, low-growth dry-cleaning equipment business. So he sought the assistance of business brokers. Maybe he could buy a more promising business.

Instead, he got a product idea. "They had some crude European devices I became interested in," says Hirsch. They were objects that looked like a mechanical shillelagh—a surgical stapler invented by a Hungarian named Hutl in 1908 and modified by a man named Von Petz. The concept was brilliant: steel staples, being chemically inert, were a safe, rapid way to close a surgical incision in an internal organ. Hutl failed because his crude stapling device was heavy and difficult to operate. It took two people two hours to assemble. Each staple had to be inserted into the machine by hand with a tweezers.

Hirsch, a tinkerer who as a child had been fond of doing things like building thermostats for his aquarium, quickly realized that modern technology could solve Hutl's problem: Use an automatic feeding cartridge for the staples. Make the stapler out of lightweight material. So Hirsch fiddled around in his basement with a balsa wood demonstration prototype and finally trotted the result around to some prominent Johns Hopkins surgeon professors.

They loved it. They offered to test a metal prototype. If it worked, they would endorse it. That was enough to induce Hirsch to invest his life savings of seventy-five thousand dollars to get metal machine shops to build working models.

The surgeons loved the prototype models. But by this point Hirsch was out of cash.

Then he got lucky. Through another surgeon to whom he had shown the models he met a wealthy lawyer named Zanvyl Krieger, a part owner of the Baltimore Orioles. Interested by this venture capital opportunity, Krieger checked back with the Johns Hopkins doctors and agreed to guarantee loans to the company up to $2 million.

The Hollywood ending does not happen here, however. At this point Hirsch took a cold hard look at his projected costs. They were all up front. If he offered the surgical stapler to major hospital distributors, he would have to have sufficient inventory on hand to meet demand, or they wouldn't carry his lines. The cost of doing that before any revenue came in was prohibitive. To cover his costs of introducing his surgical stapler, Hirsch would have to charge prices that were equally prohibitive.

---

*Don't give your new product to a distributor before you're able to meet expected demand or before you can spread your development cost over a large enough product line to price each item competitively.*

---

A less experienced businessman might have given up right there. But Hirsch figured if he had a fuller product line he could spread those same costs over more products.

It took Hirsch three full years and another $1 million to

develop a complete line of four different surgical staplers using eight different loading cartridges.

That's when the going really got rough. When he gave the product line to distributors like American Hospital Supply nothing much happened. By 1969 he was running $1 million in the red on $1 million in sales.

The doctors were buying the staplers, all right. After all, the advantages were obvious: One of Hirsch's staplers could do the equivalent of sixty-six hand-sewn sutures in five seconds—promising to cut operating time in half. That meant faster patient recovery time. The trouble was the doctors weren't using the staplers once they bought them.

Hirsch had built his business on a tip from Gillette and Kodak: Make your money on the blade, not the shaver; on the film, not the camera. In his case that translated to on the staple cartridge, not the stapler. Since the doctors weren't using the stapler, they obviously had no need for staple cartridges.

But Hirsch was not one to give up easily. They were buying the staplers, but they weren't using them. Why? Could it be that when they got into the pressure of an operating room they felt uncomfortable using a device that they hadn't learned about in medical school?

The numbers confirmed that hypothesis. The only doctors who were using the stapler on a consistent basis were the ones who had been taught how to use it during surgery by Hirsch's associate Turi Josephson. Josephson had spent two years with New York's Albert Einstein School of Medicine professors as they experimented with the staplers in the operating room. She was qualified by now as a technical expert.

This was not happy news. Hirsch had just discovered that the doctors needed major sales support, handholding, education—call it what you will. That would cost a bundle. That's assuming he could do it at all. After all, just how do you get a busy surgeon to sit still for that kind of education?

Hirsch began to realize that he needed to support his distributors with technical experts. "We needed a sales force
that could teach in addition to selling," says Hirsch. That
follow-up sales force had to have access to the surgeon
when it counted: just before the operation. That meant
they had to be technically competent enough to be hospi-
tal-qualified as experts. In other words, they had to scrub
with the surgeons and be admitted to the operating room
itself to stand by the doctor as he or she used the stapler
during the first five or six successive operations.

Registered nurses could do all that. But as assistants to a
few distributors, they turned out to be pretty expensive.
"The distributor and the nurse were spending all their time
traveling," says Hirsch. "That was expensive."

Gradually Hirsch and Josephson hit on the winning formula: Drop the distributors and use salespeople who could
also educate. They hired experienced, top notch salespeople
from various industries, put them through a rigorous training course, put them on commission—based on percentage
increase in sales—and sent them out into the nation's
operating rooms. Anyone who didn't get results quickly was
fired.

But again progress was slow. It took another ten years to
hone down the proper training course. Today U.S. Surgical
puts its salespeople through 240 hours of study, including
instruction in fifty surgical procedures, and 40 hours of animal lab training where the salesperson does the surgery
under the eye of an instructor. That gives the salesperson
hands-on experience so he or she can instruct after the sale
is made. Hirsch figures it costs his company about fifteen
thousand dollars to train a salesperson.

That's a lot for a small company, but it pays off. Operations conducted with surgical staplers have risen in number
from twenty thousand in 1969 to close to 4 million today.
Almost all U.S. medical schools teach surgical stapling

today, up from perhaps only 30 percent five years before.

Of course any product that is growing 45 percent a year and still has tapped only 20 to 25 percent of the market is bound to attract competition. Enter Johnson & Johnson, whose Ethicon division with its old-line suture business was starting to get stung by U.S. Surgical.

Hirsch says his sales force is more highly motivated and more highly trained, but competition from J & J was not something to be ignored. "We were worried," he says. "We decided if we were going to stay number one we better take them very seriously."

U.S. Surgical's response was somewhat routine: Hirsch pushed hard overseas, where surgical staplers were still a novelty, and where Johnson & Johnson was less of a competitive factor.

Then J & J began trading volleys by introducing an innovation that proved popular: the disposable surgical stapler. Soon, U.S. Surgical had a whole disposable line of its own. "They came out with a disposable skin stapler," says Hirsch. "We came out subsequently with a disposable skin stapler and a full line of internal disposables. Johnson & Johnson has been remarkably unsuccessful in trying to crack our end of the business. As of year-end 1984, we had 96 percent market share on one area where we compete. In another we have 90.2 percent. The only area where they made any significant inroads was in skin stapling, and there, believe it or not, we now have a 47 percent market share. Ethicon has 34 percent." Six other companies share the rest.

How could a little company like U.S. Surgical hold a giant like J & J to a standstill? "Better marketing. Better products," Hirsch replies. "They're trying real hard, but this is just not their specialty. They're a suture company. They don't even make their own staplers. They contract it out. Surgical stapling is all we do. Their marketing is good, but this is specialty marketing."

Not long after that, however, Hirsch stumbled badly. In 1984 the Securities and Exchange Commission charged his company with inflating its earnings from 1979 to 1981 by booking understated costs of tooling, by prematurely booking sales, by wrongly capitalizng a number of items that should have been expensed, and by failing to write off items that had been lost or scrapped. The company was forced to restate its earnings for those years.

Hirsch counters that U.S. Surgical was victimized by a former employee that the company was forced to sue at great expense. "We had a dealer who had been with us for six years, first as a salesperson and then as a dealer," Hirsch explains. "He came to us one day and said he wanted to go to Australia. He thought it was the last frontier in the Free World. He wanted to be an entrepreneur. We had essentially no business down there. He knew our business inside out. He would set up a distributorship for us down there, selling first our products exclusively, and then after he made a success of it he'd add other products.

"Well, he talked us into giving him the distributorship and financing it for him. Then he went down there and proceeded to knock off all our products. He copied everything we made and started producing the products locally. He even counterfeited our labels. We didn't find out about it until we started getting complaints that all of a sudden our products were of terrible quality."

---

*A knockoff can be just as entrepreneurial as the original— in a regional market you haven't gotten to yet.*

---

When the products were returned, Hirsch says he realized that his people had not made them.

U.S. Surgical had no patents in Australia, so Hirsch couldn't prevent his former dealer from producing, but he could proceed against him legally on charges of fraud and prevent him from copying. "We got an injunction preventing him from copying our products and requiring him to put on the product a label saying 'This is not a product of the U.S. Surgical corporation,' " Hirsch explains. "He then started selling in the U.S., and we sued him for patent infringement," he goes on.

Meanwhile the fraud suit in Australia dragged on for close to three months. "The High Court of Australia, which heard the case, upheld the fact that he had defrauded us and that there had been violations of the contract. They did not give us the business, however, only damages."

What does this have to do with the Securities and Exchange Commission? "He went to the SEC and fed them a real earful about alleged sales violations of ours," Hirsch replies. "They started investigating. It went on for two and a half years. By the time they were through they had investigated something like $400 million worth of sales between 1978 and 1981. They did come up with sales that had been booked in the wrong year. They required that that be restated. But they came up with absolutely no bogus orders or anything like that. They claim that there were improper sales practices in certain instances—alleged double shipments, things of that sort. But they conceded that customers were always given credit if they returned the shipment.

"They then started looking at accounting practices. The overwhelming majority of their complaints had to do with our accounting practices. There were ten different things they disagreed with about our accounting. Everything that they disagreed with we had already published in our annual report, and it had already been audited and signed off on by the auditors.

"For example, we had capitalized our legal expenses involving the patent suit in Australia. They said in Australia that it is a fraud suit, not a patent suit, therefore you should write it off. Had it been in the U.S., of course we would have been required to capitalize it. They went through our accounting treatment of molds and dies and said we were capitalizing improperly, even though we had specified everything we were doing ahead of time, and our auditors had agreed.

"In the end they said they wanted us to restate $28 million in earnings," says Hirsch. "Not write them off, mind you. Restate them. Different years."

It wasn't the end of the world for the company, which has recovered much of its momentum since. "Our salespeople used to tear their hair out over it, but it didn't hurt us at all in terms of our customers. In the whole U.S. I don't think we got more than fifteen or twenty letters on that whole thing," says Hirsch. "But it did cost a good $15 million in cash and it hurt our credibility."

It is ironic that the same fierce drive that enabled Hirsch to stick with his entrepreneurial vision against huge odds contributed later to sales and accounting practices that the SEC deemed excessive. Hirsch's explanation that he was betrayed by a former employee during those years evokes sympathy, but it has nothing to do with the SEC's charges. Sometimes an entrepreneur's biggest enemy can be himself.

# 8

## Thy Neighbor's Backyard

It was also someone else's bright idea that fired the imagination of Bill LeVine of Los Angeles–based Postal Instant Press. LeVine had a small commercial printing business back in the midsixties. One day in 1964 he flew to New York to pay a visit to an old high school buddy now in the garment business. In his friend John's office he saw something that fascinated him: To take pictures of his dress designs John used a new photostatic camera that Itek had developed in conjunction with Eastman Kodak. He was then able to run off copies of that picture on an offset printer in fifty-five seconds. He sent those printed copies to his potential customers. In the days of the Ditto machine and the mimeograph and the stencil that was quite a breakthrough.

"A camera!" LeVine thought to himself. Here was a two-step process instead of the nine steps needed in ordinary printing, and the quality wasn't bad. Now that might just open up a huge market that he was priced out of— those small orders for a handful of menus, brochures, or a ream of personalized stationery. It cost him so much to set up for those small orders that he had to charge more than the market was willing to pay. But with a camera like John's, "You had a $.50 cost instead of a $4.50 cost," says LeVine. "And that's not counting the savings in time,

77

labor, and everything else." It was an excellent idea that LeVine had found in his friend's backyard.

Back in Los Angeles, LeVine bought one of the forty-five-hundred-dollar cameras and started experimenting with inks, chemicals, and materials to upgrade the product. "It was a step ahead of the mimeograph, but it wasn't sale quality. It couldn't duplicate what the commercial printer could do," LeVine explains. "We played with it maybe six months to a year before putting it out in the marketplace." Pleased with the results after a year's work, he started taking small orders on the side.

Pretty soon his small-order business was growing rapidly. "The camera was making my employees nervous in the printing shop, and that was my livelihood," LeVine explains, "so I had to pull it out of there and put it in the carpeted stationery store up front surrounded by counters. That worked well because the customers could see their job being done for the first time." In 1967 he opened his first off-premise instant print shop. That in turn did so well Le-Vine opened two more.

Obviously he was on to something. A friend suggested franchising, a fever then sweeping the country. Skeptical, LeVine sold three franchises, booking a seven- to eight-thousand-dollar profit on each after the cost of buying the equipment and helping the franchisee start business.

---

*Expect heavy up-front expenditures in franchising. To finance them, go public as soon as your track record and the market permit.*

---

How could he miss? Easily, LeVine discovered. "Our franchise sells for maybe $75,000. We ask for $15,000 down. They need another, say, $20,000 operating capital in their bank account. On the tenth of the month following the day they open we pay out roughly $45,000 for the equipment, the supplies, the training, and everything else. So we've paid out $30,000 more than we've taken in." Eventually, of course, LeVine would make a handsome profit, but the more franchises he opened in the beginning the more negative his cash flow became.

Because he had to front-end the financing for his franchisees he ended up outrunning his credit line with the bank. "I couldn't do any more franchise sales because I ran out of credit. I had about forty locations back in 1969, and I had guaranteed them to the bank to get the loans. Eventually it got beyond my credit line."

Strapped for cash, LeVine listened to his broker, who suggested he sell a 20 percent stake in the company for four hundred thousand dollars to some wealthy investors the broker knew. In exchange, LeVine had to promise to make a full-fledged initial public stock offering in three or four years. It was 1969. The new-issue boom was collapsing along with the rest of the market. But investors bought in. They got lucky.

As the franchise business continued to grow and continued to need up-front capital, LeVine went public as promised. It was late January of 1973, and it was scarcely a week too soon. The stock market, worried about the pending oil embargo, plummeted.

With his financing in place, LeVine made the classic mistake of novice franchisers who are more successful than they expect to be: He was too generous in granting exclusive territories to the first franchisees. That's an easy mistake to make when you're worried about capturing the market and need all the help you can get.

"I'm not trying to say I'm normal or anything," laughs LeVine, "but I think no one starting out knows the value of their operation or how successful it's going to be. Granting exclusive franchises may have limited our market share in those regions a bit. Some owners are very happy and did not expand, but many of them have because there's no additional franchise fee, and we do 100 percent of the financing for that second location."

Those inducements are worth noting: They represent a sophisticated solution to the problem of early franchisees with giant territories who are reluctant to expand.

LeVine doesn't begrudge his early franchisees the fortunes they've made—they were the gamblers who gave him his start. They were also the stuff of dreams for his new recruits.

Why, then, is LeVine cutting back company-owned outlets from 42 to just 5 at the very time that franchise outlets are expanding at the rate of 100 a year? Older franchisors such as Holiday Inns have been doing just the opposite lately to upgrade quality standards. Is it because LeVine is making most of his money up-front—out of the franchise fee itself? "No, frankly that's one of the problems that franchising has today," LeVine replies. "People think they make most of their money from the franchise fee. But in our case the most important money is the royalty income, which generates over $1.2 million a month in earnings for us. We've got twenty-year contracts with our franchisees, and if you are taking care of that person, you are going to get more and more moola as time goes along. That's an annuity income, whereas the franchise fee is a one-time item.

"The reason we decided to cut back company-owned outlets is that we found that we couldn't be two things at the same time to the same person. We couldn't run a company operation and be franchisor as well. So we decided that we were in the instant-print franchising business now and that we would not worry about running instant-print operations. Every time we sold a company operation that location grew very fast because the owner had his own money in it. And, of course, he's not an absentee owner as is the case with many hotels."

But perhaps the greatest testimony to LeVine is that at age sixty-five, he is willing to pass the baton to a younger man with top corporate experience. At year-end 1984 he appointed Thomas C. Marotto, twenty years his junior, as chief operating officer and heir apparent. It looked like a promising choice. Marotto was a twenty-year Xerox veteran with computer marketing experience. "Yes, it's a hard decision," says LeVine. "The board wanted me to continue. But I felt that my background and my upbringing could only take us up to a certain point. My education isn't such that I can take this company further. I'm not trying to talk myself down. I think people have to know what their assets and liabilities are. Frankly, I should have done this two or three years ago. I think from this point on it will take a different kind of leadership. It will take a professional management type of leadership. When you have over a thousand locations like we do today, you can't do it the way you used to do it. I'm a hands-on guy who literally knew everything that was going on, and that frankly became impossible."

"But I'm having difficulty," he admits. "You build a company, and it's like a child. And the child is still around. At one time everyone was coming into your office, and now they're not coming in and you want to know what's going on. But you bite your lip and say, 'Let them do it.' "

Advice? "You've got to be a gambler, I guess," says LeVine. "I'm no genius. I'm not a whole lot different from the guy down the street. But I will take chances. And I'm willing to make mistakes to find the right way somewhere down the line. Instant Print wasn't a new invention. It was an obvious need. I never doubted the need for it. The mistakes were in the people, some of the marketing strategies—trying to be all things to all people. I think anyone starting a business has to have a single purpose. Focus on making one improvement, not sixty. That's the important thing in a new venture. Too many people want to run before they can walk."

---

*Be satisfied with making one significant improvement in a product or service. You're bound to make mistakes just attempting one thing—many more if you try to do too much all at once.*

---

And concentrate on profits? LeVine nods his head in agreement. "I was just talking to a friend of mine," he says. "His son wants to be the biggest in his business. He wants to go nationwide. The bottom line, profits, is a secondary issue to him. I said the bottom line is the important issue, not how many millions of sales you have. You can do ten million and go broke. Do one million and make some money!"

# 9

## Me-Tooing the Mighty

It's one thing to borrow a good idea you stumbled across in your neighbor's backyard, but it's quite another for a would-be entrepreneur to borrow a good idea from the industry leader. Normally that dooms you to the narrow-margined world of cheap knockoffs and discounting.

But for some entrepreneurs who really think through their corporate strategy, copying a good idea from the industry leader can make excellent sense. Take a company like Brenco of Petersburg, Virginia, which serves a slow-moving basic industry: Railroads.

Brenco was just a little job-shop railroad foundry back in 1958 when it decided to compete head-to-head with mighty Timken by copying a Timken innovation called the tapered roller bearing.

Now it was clear that the tapered bearing would outlast the then-standard bronze straight bearing by a country mile because it spread the wear and tear over more bearing surface area as the car moved. But it was not at all clear how Brenco could hope to compete with Timken.

Me-tooing the mighty in a capital-intensive industry? Most businessmen would call that madness, not entrepreneurial.

Most businessmen would have been wrong. Brenco's founder Needham Whitfield knew that the railroads, like

Detroit auto makers, understandably hated to rely on just one supplier for a critical part. That would just invite that supplier to raise his prices.

So Whitfield had spotted a genuine market. The railroads would buy bearings from another manufacturer, however small, just so they didn't have to depend solely on Timken.

But there was also a problem even more obvious than that market: without Timken's fully integrated specialty steelmaking and fabricating capacity, how could anyone possibly compete with it on price? And how could Brenco possibly duplicate that fabricating and steelmaking capacity without inconceivably large up-front capital expenditures?

Such sensible questions would have stopped many businessmen. But Brenco entered the tapered roller bearing business with rented machinery and very limited capacity. From long industry experience, Brenco's Whitfield figured the railroads would be slow in switching to the newfangled bearings, just as they'd been slow switching to new technology for decades. To the railroads, new technology just meant big expense and a chance to make a mistake. Why bother being innovative? No one else was going to take their market away in their then-regulated industry.

---

*No customer wants to be entirely dependent on just one supplier, no matter who it is. Ask yourself what your competitor's customers want. Better yet, ask them.*

---

Whitfield also figured Timken would be reluctant to lower prices on its own innovation before the market was fully established. Like most manufacturers, accustomed to a leading market share position, Timken was used to holding a price umbrella over smaller competitors. Timken knew it was much easier to lower the price than to raise it back up again later.

Whitfield was right on both counts. So gradual was the growth in demand for tapered roller bearings that Brenco had time to integrate backward into all phases of fabrication in easily self-financed stages—steadily improving its costs in a growing market. And Timken prices held steady for years, just as Whitfield had predicted. By 1980 Brenco was earning $15 million on sales of over $88 million with no debt for a handsome 30 percent return on equity. Its 9.8 million shares were trading at twenty-five, sixteen times earnings—well above the market average. That was the payoff for a brilliant marketing insight, superbly supported with a bold capital spending program that took considerable management self-discipline to execute.

But then the bottom fell out. By 1984 Brenco was running in the red on not even 25 percent of its 1980 sales volume. Its shares were trading at five.

What went wrong? Brenco's market fell apart. The newly deregulated railroads had been flat on their backs for five years straight and just hadn't been buying new equipment. Brenco has been a key casualty. Already larger than Timken in railroad roller bearings, it had allowed itself to be far too concentrated in one market. The company will survive, thanks mainly to its debt-free balance sheet. But that is cold comfort to investors who spotted what an excellent little company it was in palmier days and never sold. In hindsight they should have been asking the skeptical questions venture capitalists are noted for, like, "How long will the railroad equipment market stay this strong?"

More to the point, Brenco management should have been asking those skeptical questions when return on equity was running at a hard-to-maintain 30 percent. At that point, with the wind full at its back, it should have been taking steps to lessen dependence on the railroad market.

Brenco is the first to admit it. In a masterpiece of southern understatement Brenco Chairman and Chief Executive George Copeland, brought in from Swedish ball-bearing giant SKF in 1979, puts it this way: "I guess if we had our druthers, we would have been a lot less dependent on the railroad equipment business than we are."

In fairness, of course, it takes more discipline than most of us possess to slow down when things are going well. After all, from a standing start Brenco had locked horns with mighty Timken, a near monopoly, and won in one of its key markets.

The point is no matter how brilliant the initial insight and no matter how painstaking and thoughtful the execution, there comes a time when you have to protect your flanks. All markets change, and that change can happen quickly. You must be prepared.

That may sound obvious. But in the day-to-day rush of a successful business it's easy to forget that just when things are really going well is when you should prepare for uncertainty. Thomas Watson, IBM's founder, understood this. He never tired of saying that companies don't get in trouble during recessions; they get in trouble during prosperity. Brenco never learned that. The caution that served it so well in its early days was thrown away when business was booming.

# 10

## "The Gravy Doesn't Last Forever"

It's always a good idea to ask yourself, "What if something goes wrong?" if only because it keeps reminding you that nothing lasts forever. If you take the trouble to answer the question, you'll have some sort of fallback when trouble strikes.

Take the case of Shopsmith, whose market didn't sour—it just wasn't very big to start with.

Merrill Lynch stockbroker John Folkerth of Dayton, Ohio, was a hobbyist woodworker back in 1971 when he got the idea of buying the rights to the defunct Shopsmith multipurpose woodworking tool—a combination table saw, lathe, horizontal boring machine, disk sander, and vertical drill press all in one. Any woodworker worth his sawdust knew how handy it was in a crowded basement. So imagine Folkerth's surprise when he tried to buy a new blade for the tool and discovered that the product line had been discontinued. With a little more attention to marketing the product would surely be a winner, he thought. He was further encouraged when the company that used to make the device showed him a thick stack of mail from do-it-yourselfers and hardware store owners all wondering when the Shopsmith would be back on the market. For just $250,000 Folkerth could buy the rights and go into business for himself.

After six months of hard work raising money, Folkerth

was in business. Two years later he was on top of the world, shipping the tool to two hundred dealers and making ten thousand dollars a month.

Then came the first sign of trouble. The dealers had been ordering far more Shopsmiths than they had been selling. Now they were beginning to send them back. Folkerth had to write off some of his profits. But he refused to believe that he had overestimated the size of the market. He was using an old-fashioned distribution channel, he told himself. Suburbanites were increasingly shopping at shopping malls, not isolated hardware stores. So Folkerth set up demonstration Shopsmith stands in malls, his salespeople performing all manner of woodworking tricks for prospective customers. It clicked. Sales climbed, and even better, now Folkerth was selling direct to the consumer, improving his profit margins by cutting out the retail middleman. When Shopsmith went public in 1979 Folkerth was able to produce sensational numbers: a five-year average earnings-per-share growth rate of 72 percent, a return on equity of 34 percent. Long-term debt was down to just 16 percent of book value. But by 1985 Shopsmith had been running in the red for four of the past five years.

What went wrong? First, what looked like a perfectly logical product extension merger went sour. "We made an acquisition five years ago that was nicely profitable in its first year, and after that it was a real drain," Folkerth says. "The company was Benchmark, which was in the small stationary tool market. We shouldn't have been in it because it got blown to hell by the Taiwanese. We finally got out of it in 1984. We would have been profitable without that."

But why weren't Shopsmith's profits enough to at least offset this? The overvalued dollar made imports cheap. A Taiwanese knockoff came on the market at half the price of the Shopsmith. Folkerth's own customers were soon writing him letters about it, warning that some of his dealers were undercutting him. But in a larger sense, Folkerth's basic problem was skimming. He had quickly saturated a limited market for his product—for the second time. "I couldn't argue with that," says Folkerth. "If you're right, of course, then the Taiwanese are skimming too. Our guess is that if we had their share of the market as well as ours we'd be within 90 percent of what our peak was. What generally happens is we go in and sell the unit, and then they come in with a cheaper price and fulfill the order.

"The other thing is that there is also a flood of cheap Taiwanese stationary tools coming into the market. I think that has expanded our market because all the retailers from K-Mart to Pier One have them. But again it has also taken market away from other established sellers like Sears or Montgomery Ward. It's kind of like smoking, you know. When I was smoking I used to say to myself 'I don't know if this is bad for me or not, but I can't believe it's good for me!'"

---

*Anyone can fall into the skimming trap by overestimating the market. Keep sounding for the bottom.*

---

So what is Folkerth doing about it? "Well, let's put it this way," he replies. "I just got back from Taiwan! We're going to start having them make parts for us. We've got to get our costs down—we had a major layoff. But, frankly, anyone who investigates hard enough can buy everything we've got at two-thirds the price. They may not get the quality, but they can do it."

Does Folkerth think that his predecessor, who cashed in his chips, experienced the same plateauing of his market? "Very possibly," he replies. "They very possibly ran out of growth in their marketing channel like we ran out of growth in ours. We do direct-mail and magazine advertisements. But at this point we can't put any more ads in

magazines and have productive results. We can't go to any
more malls and get productive results. So the marketing
channels we have presently identified are mature. We are
working on some more, but they have not proven out as
yet."

Couldn't Folkerth go overseas? "Every time we get
geared up and get ready to go, we run into a domestic
problem and have to abort," he replies. "Of course, the past
couple of years wouldn't have been any good anyway because of the dollar."

What has Folkerth learned from all this? "One, the gravy
doesn't last forever!" he says. "No matter how brilliant you
are, you're not going to keep growing at those kind of com-
pounded rates. I was naive and allowed our overheads to
balloon because I thought I would have another two years.
I didn't get it. When I realized that, I was not fast or ruthless enough in pulling back. We had 550 people, and we
had to let 100 go and shut down the plant for three weeks
to bring our inventories in line. It's hard.

"Another thing I've learned is that Shopsmith as a manufacturer was not attuned to what the imports were doing
to us. I also did not perceive the public is willing to pay
only so much for premium quality. Thanks to the last recession the premium they'll pay is only 15 to 20 percent. If
it gets above that, then the people will not buy.

"I also think that any manufactured product today is
going to be judged in terms of the value people get from
other manufactured products whether they compete with
you or not. Because of the tremendous lowering of the
prices of other manufactured products they're starting to
get a general feel that 'Hey, these things should be a lot
cheaper than this.' "

Today, a leaner Shopsmith will soon be looking for a new
product line. "But we've neglected our basic product line,
so we're going to make that solid before we begin playing
the diversification game again."

A venture capitalist would point out that Folkerth could have saved himself a lot of trouble at a critical moment in Shopsmith's early years if he had taken the trouble to draw up a sound business plan. One of the first things a venture capitalist would have looked for in such a plan is how Folkerth estimated the probable size of his market. Chances are Folkerth's seat-of-the-pants estimates would not have passed muster.

Skimming, in other words, is one trap that can often be avoided by a good business plan that takes careful soundings of the anticipated market.

That doesn't mean that Folkerth's idea should have been abandoned. But a better plan would have thrown the spotlight at the outset on a question that Folkerth still hasn't addressed: whether he really is an entrepreneur—or just a very clever investor who is able to spot undervalued assets.

If John Folkerth had realized in the beginning that he was likely to saturate his original market quickly, he could have reinvested those early spectacular earnings and launched an entrepreneurial follow-on product, or at least made a soundly conceived acquisition.

Now Folkerth has to attempt that when his glory days are over, and against much stiffer competition from abroad. He has less time and less capital than might otherwise have been the case. It is a galling realization.

# 11

## Cream, Glorious Cream

If the industry is big enough, of course, you don't really have to worry *as much* about the danger of skimming a market that's really too small for you.

Take automobile insurance, for example. With skyrocketing auto repair costs and medical bills, auto insurance companies have often in recent years paid out more in expenses than they have received in premiums.

If that were your backyard, do you think you could find opportunity there? Lou Foster of Twentieth Century Insurance did. A onetime Detroit door-to-door appliance salesman, and later a remarkably successful independent insurance agent, Foster was convinced an insurance company could very profitably eliminate the middle man—insurance agents like himself. Agents didn't really do anything significant for their clients once they'd sold them insurance coverage—nothing, that is, that an insurance company wasn't already doing itself. The trick was for insurance companies to find qualified customers.

As an agent back in the thirties, he had learned that only one out of fifteen people could land a job at the local telephone company or other utilities. So all he had to do was concentrate on trying to sell those employees insurance, and he would be concentrating on the lowest risks. His results spoke for themselves over the next twenty years.

So why not offer insurance only to the lowest-risk automobile drivers? You didn't need a computer to pick out the characteristics you'd want—mature, stable people with good jobs who drove conservative cars. The confirmation was right there in the statistics from Foster's thirteen-hundred-person client list.

Then why not sell to them direct—without agents? The selling point was obvious: price. With a big insurance company that didn't bother to distinguish between low and high risk there was one uniform rate. Concentrating on low-risk customers meant considerably lower costs. Selling to them direct, without salespeople-agents, did too. So Foster could offer his old clients insurance at a significantly lower price—around 20 percent to 30 percent off.

The good news is that all but one of Foster's original clients switched their auto insurance to him in 1958 when he started Twentieth Century Insurance.

The bad news is that, in the beginning at least, growing by word of mouth can be a very slow process for a highly selective business. It took Twentieth Century ten years to do $1 million in sales.

---

*He who ignores the past of his own industry is doomed to repeat its classic mistakes in the present. Conversely, he who reads his history can learn lessons that will work over and over again.*

---

But by the early eighties, Twentieth Century was as profitable and fast growing as an entrepreneur could wish for, thanks to expenses that run only 91 cents of every premium dollar and investment earnings of $5 million pretax. Currently, with over $200 million in sales, Twentieth Century is earning more than a 20 percent return on equity. After the worst period in recent memory for the property and casualty industry, those numbers look outstanding. But Twentieth Century President G. Robert Thompson dreams of a return to 40 percent returns on equity.

Foster's concept was hardly a new idea. GEICO [Government Employees Insurance Company] has done it for decades—letting the government cull out a vast pool of stable insurance prospects for it. Now USAA, giant retailer J. C. Penney, and a host of other companies are copying this marketing strategy.

In other words, one of the basic problems with purposeful skimming in a business as big as insurance is that you are bound to attract competition when your competitors read your annual reports and see how profitable your approach is. Nor does your niche protect you from the general pressures of the industry, such as skyrocketing jury awards, which your larger competitors may be much better able to deal with than you.

It is worth noting that for the first time Twentieth Century began advertising in the summer of 1984.

Would the discipline of drawing up a sound business plan have predicted that the salad days of Twentieth Century Insurance wouldn't last forever? Would such a business plan have emphasized far earlier the need to develop new strategies at an earlier date? It certainly wouldn't have hurt.

# 12

## The Grass Looks Greener

The way entrepreneurs like Folkerth and Foster get trapped into skimming, aside from overestimating the size of their market, is the very sensible fear of taking on too much. Even experienced entrepreneurs often become overextended. They see too many opportunities for their own good and end up spreading themselves too thin.

John Grove could tell you that. He had built up a very successful business making small hydraulic cranes and in 1967 sold it to conglomerate Walter Kidde for $27 million. With his share of the proceeds, close to $5 million, he dabbled in real estate and got nowhere. Frustrated, he and his wife drove around visiting former Grove crane dealers looking for opportunities in related markets. They found one that was similar to the industrial cranes he'd made but not so similar as to violate his no-compete clause with Kidde. Instead of building something to lift construction materials, his former dealers asked, why not build something to lift people? So Grove came up with a new product line: low-slung telescoping-boom or scissors-lift work platforms with the controls out on the platform itself for convenience. Grove's original concept was to sell them to the industrial maintenance market.

Soon he bought a local sheet metal fabricator, called it JLG Industries, and started building "cherry picker" work platforms. When he took the finished product on the road it won instant acceptance, thanks in no small part to his own successful track record in the business.

By 1980 JLG had over half the market for telescoping work platforms and 10 percent of the older scissors-lift work platforms. Grove's numbers looked terrific: a return on equity the year before of 22.2 percent on sales of over $60 million. And that was despite sharply higher capital spending of $13 million, up from $3 million. JLG common hit 22½, seventeen times earnings—far above the market averages.

Then everything fell apart. For the next three years straight JLG ran in the red, despite promising new products. JLG common sank from 22½ to 4½, when it traded at all.

What went wrong? Grove was lured away from his original target market, the industrial maintenance business, by easy sales to the then-booming construction market, in which the little work platform lifts were ideal for the upper-level work on low-rise commercial construction. By 1980 almost three-quarters of his sales volume was to the construction trades. But the construction business is fickle, being fueled chiefly by the money its prospective customers are able to borrow and, more importantly, by the interest rates they will have to pay. Says Grove: "It was just too damned easy. I got too damned busy cranking out those machines for the construction guys. My original idea, the industrial market, was the right one."

# 13

## Fads, Fashions, and Things That Go Bump in the Night

Profits from products that are subject to fads and fashions are just as green as those made from making railroad roller bearings or telescoping work platforms. But managing the marketing and production of such products can be quite tricky. How do you get the most out of a fashion item without allowing it to bury you?

Don't think that's a question reserved mainly for those in the clothing business. You may be in the fad-and-fashion game without even knowing it.

Consider the plight of National Lampoon, whose flagship magazine of the same name once put a stray dog on its cover with the caption "If you don't buy this magazine, we'll shoot this dog!" Founded in 1970, the magazine was strong on political and sick humor that struck a responsive chord with the World War II baby boomers then in college.

But today most college students are more worried about getting into the M.B.A. program at Wharton than they are about protesting foreign wars. "Politics is just not something people like to laugh about now," concedes Chairman Matty Simmons.

In hopes of extracting a new brand of humor from new blood, Simmons replaced the magazine's entire staff in early 1984.

Meanwhile other parts of the business were peaking, like their much-heralded move into movies. *Animal House,* which featured food fights, voyeurism, and the widespread destruction of public property, may have been one of the best-grossing films of all time. But most of what has followed proved disappointing. While National Lampoon's *Summer Vacation,* starring ex-Lampoon staffer Chevy Chase, did do well, National Lampoon's *Reunion* bombed, and three other movies, *National Lampoon Goes to the Movies, National Lampoon's Joy of Sex,* and *Animal House II,* were never even released.

---

*If you're in a fashion business—and you may be, without knowing it—the crucial marketing knowledge is what's hot and for how long. The only known way to answer that is to keep asking.*

---

The problem is National Lampoon's brand of humor now seems dated to its core-collegiate market, traditionally one of the most fickle around. To collegians it was a fad whose time is past. Just ask any formerly hot fashion designer about Matty Simmons's chances of catching the current brand of humor on campus as well as he did ten years ago.

# 14

## The Flash in the Pan

Isadore "Hack" Miller of Rival Manufacturing knows about the odds of repeating a fad product's success. In the midseventies Rival Manufacturing hit it big with its Rival Crock Pot. From 1972 to 1976, Rival averaged a stunning 49 percent return on equity with little long-term debt, thanks to its slow-cooking Crock Pot. By 1976 Rival common was trading at thirty-six, after 1975 earnings hit $23 million on sales of $126 million.

But just two years later Rival common was selling as low as seven, as earnings dropped to less than $6 million. Things kept deteriorating. In 1983 Rival lost $4 million, after taking a substantial inventory write-off on Japanese-made kerosene heaters.

Why wasn't Rival's President Miller able to capitalize on the stunning success of the Crock Pot? After all, he had two seemingly excellent opportunities. He had a prototype food processor before the emergence of Cuisinart, and he had a premium-priced coffee maker before Mr. Coffee came on the scene. Why didn't Miller try to use the coattails of the Crock Pot to launch those promising products?

Looking back, Miller, seventy-nine, concedes he probably underestimated what the market was willing to pay for such products. Long accustomed to operating on thin margins, and with long-suffering shareholders finally in clover, he was reluctant to spoil a good thing.

And he had his hands full just putting out fires on the Crock Pot. In short order, Miller had to contend with (1) overcoming an initial 80 percent reject rate in pottery liners supplied for the Crock Pot; (2) watching receivables like a hawk to guard against dealer overordering; (3) coping with a major fire at a supplier's plant; (4) trying to rush out add-on products for the Crock Pot line before they were ready; (5) having to dissipate capital by paying out huge dividends to controlling outside shareholders when by all odds he should have been plowing the proceeds back into the business; and then (6) having to eat huge amounts of inventory as sales nosedived in 1976.

In retrospect Hack Miller says he thinks Rival did very well to survive the Crock Pot, much less capitalize on its success. A veteran of many years as a housewares buyer at New York's Macy's department store, Miller knew countless horror stories of manufacturers who got carried away with a hot product, only to go out of business a few years later.

As a result of that conservative streak, Crock Pot, which might have been the cornerstone of a housewares empire, became just a flash in the pan.

# 15

## Fluke

Hack Miller had other arrows in his quiver when he hit it big with the Crock Pot. But rightly or wrongly, he just didn't feel he had the resources or a good enough target at which to fire them.

Compare that with Wells Gardner, which had an empty quiver. Wells Gardner thought the video game craze was the answer to its prayers. And for two years it was.

A private-label manufacturer of television sets, the Chicago company fell on hard times when lower-price Japanese sets swept the market in the midseventies. "We were barely hanging on by our fingernails," concedes President Albert Wells. Wells Gardner lost money for five years straight. Then the video games hoopla hit, and Wells Gardner took its television chassis, fiddled a bit, and shazam! It had a video game monitor.

Sales quadrupled between 1979 and 1981, and the stock did even better. But then the video game craze went the way of the hula hoop. Sales fell 63 percent between 1982 and 1983. By 1984 the company was running in the red.

"I can't think of anything else I could have done," says Wells today. "I guess what we learned was that forecasting is impossible. I knew it would end, but we didn't get our feet in the door fast enough with data display monitors, our next product."

To give Wells his due, just when video games were hottest, his research people were feverishly working on data display monitors for computers and other lines. "It took us longer to get our name established for that product in the marketplace than we expected. We thought we could do it in a year. It took two."

Also to his credit, Wells has survived a shakeout that saw the number of video game suppliers fall from around forty to six. He's still on top in that market. But obviously it avails little when the market itself has collapsed. So Wells has moved on. In addition to making display monitors for computer manufacturers, he is looking at state lotteries marketed over video monitors and point-of-purchase video monitors in grocery stores.

What advice would Wells give to his fellow entrepreneurs?

"Cut the forecast in half!" he says.

# 16

## There Is Nothing Like a Niche

The classic entrepreneurial defense to perils of the sort we've been describing is to seek out a "niche"—usually a market too small for larger competitors to bother with.

Becoming the big frog in such a small pond can make you what *Forbes* magazine used to call a "baby blue chip"—a company blessed with a profitability as formidable in its market as an IBM, General Electric or a Pillsbury.

Twenty years ago the concept was so well known that conglomerates were built on clearing up the estates of baby blue-chip founders. Textron, founded by Royal Little and brilliantly redefined by Rhode Island banker Rupert Thompson, was in the sixties and early seventies perhaps the best-known collection of baby blue chips around.

There is no more sensible strategy we can think of for tomorrow's entrepreneur than to try to find and master a niche. But that is easier said than done. Everyone is looking for niches, which are now widely recognized as potentially more lucrative and far safer than many large markets.

Warren Musser of Safeguard Scientific knows how difficult it is to find a niche. Few entrepreneurs have tried harder to find someone else's niche than miniconglomerateur Musser. The irony is that he created one himself without even realizing it for many years.

He started on his quixotic quest back in the midfifties as a twenty-seven-year-old boy-wonder stockbroker investing three hundred thousand dollars of his clients' money in cable television. The idea was great, but the timing wasn't. Musser was years ahead of the market. Musser grossly underestimated the amount of money he'd have to spend up front to install the cable.

---

*A niche is usually a product that is not glamorous but is nevertheless indispensable to a limited market. They can be easy to miss.*

---

Nine years later, in 1963, Musser sold out and invested what was left in a tiny, marginal business forms company he had been running on the side with his former college roommate, Vincent G. "Buck" Bell. At the time, about all you could say for the company was that it had been available. Its checkwriting machines were outmoded and lasted forever. Its forms were little more than a commodity. But that vehicle was enough to attract a stock market–savvy man like Musser at the beginnings of one of the longest bull markets in history—a bull market that was to be fueled primarily by the conglomeration craze.

But before he set out to outshine the great conglomerateurs of the day, Musser did two things that were to top anything he did before or has done since. He introduced a folding combination check book/ledger book. The checks had carbon strips on the back that duplicated all disbursements on record paper beneath. For a small shopkeeper, it was a one-book daily log that updated itself automatically—an invaluable assist.

As innovations go, that was admittedly small potatoes. But they are small potatoes that reappear every spring. Get enough of them, and you eat well.

But Musser had his sights set higher than trying to be-

come IBM on one-hundred-dollar orders. If Gulf & Western had started out in the high-margin replacement auto
parts business, then he would too. So he bought the Hub
City Iron Company of Aberdeen, South Dakota. They
made automobile hubcaps.

Wall Street went wild. Equity Research, then a particularly well regarded group of Wall Street analysts, had said
something about liking Safeguard's accounting system—
referring to Musser's notebooks—and investors thought the
reference was to Safeguard as a whole. That was in 1967 at
the height of a roaring bull market. As Safeguard Industries stock hit forty times earnings, Musser used that grossly
inflated market value to buy assets cheap—the standard
conglomerateur ploy. He bought a cross-section of the Lil-
liputian Rust Belt: a little valve company, a tiny pump
company, a small industrial power transmission company,
and a computer service bureau.

Three years later Musser was on a roll with a return on
equity in the high teens and $70 million in sales. Then the
market just came to a stop. Safeguard's earnings faltered.
Musser regretted he hadn't gone after larger acquisitions
that would have given him staying power. He'd been afraid
of diluting his own small 8 percent ownership position too
much.

Not until the midseventies did Musser finally realize the
gold mine he had in his own backyard. Those little notebooks of his kept growing, slowly but surely, every year
compounding on repeat business. In fact, hard as it was to
admit it, they were supporting the whole company.

One reason that business was doing so well was that its
salespeople had an excellent incentive borrowed from the
insurance industry. They got to pocket the profits from all
the repeat business on any sale they made. That tended to
attract experienced salespeople, people with enough savings to tide them over the early building years. But all this

was obscured by the high leverage of the parent company and the low profitability of the other subsidiaries.

Then in 1980 Musser did an interesting thing: He spun off the folding notebook business to his long-suffering shareholders with his friend Buck Bell at the helm. Under the name Safeguard Business Systems it has flourished with the predictability of spring wheat. Since year-end 1979, earnings nearly doubled from $6.4 million to $11 million within four years. Return on shareholder equity, though down from its impossible-to-maintain pre-spin-off high of 50 percent, was running above 25 percent, a distinctly superior performance. The folding notebook line has mushroomed to more than two thousand items and has expanded to include computerized services for accountants and businessmen. Buck Bell has now bought his way into microcomputer and software distribution for larger corporate clients and computer-aided instruction programs.

As for Warren Musser, he's still trying in vain to bring back the opportunity he thinks he missed in the sixties. By selling off subsidiaries, he has produced a fairly clean balance sheet for Safeguard Industries. Then he renamed the company Safeguard Scientifics to signal his new acquisitive interests: taking investment positions in emerging growth companies in the sciences that are supported by established cash-generating businesses. But the established companies haven't been able to generate the cash any more than the emerging companies have been able to generate the growth. After the first four years, Scientifics lost $10 million in stockholder equity and doubled its debt since then.

But at least Musser didn't hang on to Safeguard Business Systems and use its predictable earnings to cover up his mistakes.

# 17

## "Nobody Wants to Clean a Parts Cleaner"

Lest you think that the folding notebooks of Safeguard Business Systems are in any way unique, consider the closely similar niche of the highly successful Safety Kleen Corp. Like Business System's notebooks, Safety Kleen's basic product is a mundane, small-ticket item: a parts-cleaning service for gas stations, body shops, and factories. Like Business Systems, Safety Kleen has a very large number of small customers who renew regularly. And like Business Systems, that gives Safety Kleen a built-in market for add-on merchandise, which both have capitalized on beautifully.

---

*Big corporations need quick results so their chief executives can show rising earnings. They usually don't have the patience to grow a niche.*

---

Niches of this sort only improve with age. Their value, like fine wines, can be measured by the time it takes to mature them. Major corporations rarely feel they can wait that long for a significant impact on the bottom line.

But many in the executive ranks of big corporations eye little niche companies with considerable envy. That's why smallish companies with a leading position in slow-growing but reliable markets have been targets in the current rash of leveraged buyouts.

If those same executives had had the courage and the foresight to buy into that niche before it became so obvious, it would have cost them far less, and they could have made a real contribution to the company's future, instead of crippling it with debt in a leveraged buyout.

But spotting a niche before it's obvious is tricky. Take Safety Kleen, for example. Like Warren Musser, Safety Kleen's Don Brinckman stumbled upon his niche by accident. Back in 1968 Brinckman was working for a company called Chicago Rawhide that made oil seals, washers, and gaskets and was dying on the vine. Brinckman was running the replacement parts side of the business and was looking for small acquisitions. One day a business broker suggested he look at Safety Kleen.

SK didn't look too prepossessing back then. Top-heavy with debt, it was running fifty thousand dollars in the red on just fifty thousand dollars in sales, cranking out a simple little product anyone could have duplicated in half a day. It was nothing more than a washtub with a spigot that directed a stream of solvent onto the dirty part to be washed and then recycled the solvent through a filter into a nearby drum. Every few months the solvent was replaced.

Unlike Musser, Brinckman spotted the potential niche right away—possibly because he was hungrier, and possibly because as a former market research consultant he had an eye for it. "We were not that impressed by the company, but they had about four hundred to five hundred outlets on a route operation, and when we went around and talked to their customers they were very enthusiastic about it," says Brinckman. "That immediately triggered the thought that if they liked it here in Milwaukee, well, maybe they'd like it everywhere. We saw it on a national basis right away, although we never realized we could build it into something this large. We thought the parts-cleaning business probably could end up with something like fifty thousand customers and serve as a base for either marketing directly or for our distributors. So we bought it in about two weeks."

Why would a service station care about Safety Kleen's little washtub? Because solvent is highly flammable, no gas station owner wanted his mechanics leaving buckets of dirty solvent and solvent-soaked rags lying about all the time. "A lot of them were using gasoline to clean their parts, and that is really dangerous," notes Brinckman. Service station owners also didn't like having to throw out another bucketful of the dangerous solvent or gasoline every time their mechanics washed off a grimy auto part. SK's tub recycled that solvent and shielded the worker from fire by slamming shut automatically should a blaze melt the metal latch holding up its heavy cover. That metal latch had a very low melting point.

As mundane as this sounds, it was a truly first-rate entrepreneurial opportunity. In time SK could give the solvent replacement salespeople more products to offer on their regular rounds. So Chicago Rawhide bought SK for a song—$25,000 cash down, and an agreement to pick up SK's $160,000 in debt.

Brinckman put his entire nationwide sales force behind the product right away, using temporary help as well.

"We divided the country up into about 130 potential routes, each with the same potential as Milwaukee, grouped them into seven regions, hired regional managers, and began a blitz. That meant literally going down the street and putting in our product free for anyone who would try it. Then a week or two later we'd come back and see if they wanted to sign up for the service." The product literally sold itself on sight. "It really filled a need," says Brinckman. "The worst part about parts cleaning is that when a parts cleaner gets dirty, it really gets dirty! And nobody wants to clean a parts cleaner. So what we were doing was taking away all the dirt. We brought back clean solvent. They never had to get involved with cleaning the parts cleaner."

---

*Seek out an industry's dirty work. People don't see it as an opportunity. It can be.*

---

Nearly 90 percent of the gas stations he showed it to bought it. But it was an easy idea to steal, and Brinckman knew it. "We thought the best thing to do was to get into as many markets as we could as fast as we could," he says. "We wanted to preclude any competitor from getting a foothold in any one regional market. That meant we couldn't start regionally ourselves. If we did, then some guy would have started it on the West Coast and some other guy in Florida. So we really moved quite rapidly. We bought the company on October first, and we started our first blitz on November first. We had to set up systems, get trucks, and recruit people all in four weeks."

Next Brinckman moved to consolidate his ground. He offered to resupply solvent for any gas station whether it had SK's parts cleaner or not. Then the SK service representative could use those regular service calls to sell oil seals, filters, wiper blades, or any other auto aftermarket product. He could sell those products for less because he was selling direct.

As the business grew, however, the cost of disposing of a hazardous waste like used solvent began to grow at an alarming rate. But that was to become a blessing in disguise. "It is now regulated by the Environmental Protection Agency, which is a big plus for our parts-cleaning service," says Brinckman.

"At that point we were buying solvent at about fifteen cents a gallon, very cheaply. We looked at recycling right away because we knew we were going to end up with an awful lot of dirty solvent, and what were we going to do with it? We figured it was going to cost us probably about fifteen to twenty cents to recycle because you have an awful lot of freight. We were operating on a shoestring at the time. But then our supplier, Shell Oil, offered to sell us one of its old plants for just the price of the underlying land— fifteen thousand dollars. That would lower our costs substantially. So we put about seventy-five thousand dollars' worth of equipment into it and started to learn about recycling." Brinckman then built other plants in New Jersey and the West Coast.

Then came the Arab oil embargo of 1973. At this point Brinckman had three recycling plants operating. Solvent prices, along with petroleum prices, doubled. Then they tripled again. Meanwhile, Brinckman's recycling costs barely doubled. Brinckman found himself sitting pretty.

Today Safety Kleen recycles 92 percent of its dirty solvent, saving millions, the result of that unlikely decision to recycle. "We really had no economic incentive to recycle," Brinckman concedes. "But that decision has made a major difference in our business."

There were setbacks of course. Gas stations had a hard time of it in the late seventies and early eighties, many thousands of them closing their doors for good each year. But Brinckman had already gone overseas, which compensated to some extent. And in 1979 he had gone after new markets like restaurants—where Safety Kleen took care of the ever-greasy exhaust filters from the kitchen. Never once did he forget that Safety Kleen's strength is its ability to handle small orders efficiently.

"Originally we got into restaurants because one of the fast-food chains was trying to clean its filters in one of our parts cleaners," Brinckman explains. "Soon it was apparent that you couldn't clean filters that way. Then we thought if there's a problem cleaning filters, maybe there's a better way to do it. We developed a filter you wouldn't have to clean. It's aluminum and can be recycled. We actually bring new filters in each time. We stamp them out at our plant, bring them back when they're dirty, compress them, and throw them into an aluminum recycling plant."

In 1979, sporting a better than 35 percent return on equity with low debt and a splendid track record—sales and earnings having tripled over the past five years—Brinckman went public.

Related market opportunities opened up gradually. "We purchased a small company that was doing the same thing we were with buffing pads," says Brinckman. "Auto repair body shops were using them to buff paint jobs. Usually they just threw the old buffing pad away because it was all clogged up with paint. This company was leasing buffing pads and encouraging customers to change them often, which really speeds up the job. They would then process the pads and return them to the body shop. They were doing the same thing with pads that we were doing with solvent. So we bought them and broadened the line. That business has increased 500 percent since then."

That of course helped offset the saturation that was happening in the original gas station parts-cleaning business. Another thing that helped was capitalizing on SK's waste disposal technology. "By now we have probably become the world's leading solvent recycler," says Brinckman.

"I think one of our advantages was that all our recycling plants were situated to serve our branches. Good logistical structure. And we bought enough land that we could expand. I think that has helped us tremendously because freight is the biggest cost factor in recycling.

"Now the government has dramatically lowered the level

of hazardous waste a business outlet can generate without filing a manifest—from one thousand kilograms down to one hundred. That has opened up hundreds of thousands of outlets that were just throwing their stuff in the garbage. Dry-cleaning shops are an example. We pick up their waste, recycle that, and get the perchlorethylene out of it."

For dry-cleaning shops, Safety Kleen offered the lowest-cost alternative. To burn that waste or put it in a landfill would cost more.

---

*If you think big in terms of market growth, think big early in terms of logistical support: Buy enough land. Build plants as regional hubs for your markets.*

---

Safety Kleen's earnings tripled again in just four more years. And despite two splits the stock has risen steadily from around ten to over forty—better than twenty-one times earnings and well above the market average.

There is an easy moral to draw from Brinckman's success. "Right from the start we laid out a pretty good cash-flow projection, and I don't think we could have done it without doing that exercise," says Brinckman. "The first year we did a million in sales, but lost a million too, and required almost three million more in capital. If we hadn't had that cash-flow requirement figured out, we never would have been able to operate the second year. You have tremendous start-up costs, and you're only getting a very little bit for each service. You have to get a pretty good base before you can start to make any money in this business."

That kind of analysis, of course, is precisely what a business plan asks of a would-be entrepreneur.

# 18

## The Disappearing Niche

Time was when the mere mention of the words *specialty chemical* connoted niche. But the word got around. Today, if you want to be profitable in specialty chemicals, you have to be the market leader. The larger component markets in specialty chemicals were generating enough business to attract the big chemical companies. The niche outgrew itself. It has become sufficiently large to attract larger competition, driving the former entrepreneurs back into its innumerable component markets, where much smaller niches continue to survive.

But sometimes those fallback niches are hard to find. Consider, for example, the interesting case of CPT, a producer of stand-alone word processors. Dean Scheff, founder of CPT and a former personal computer dealer, knew that many big companies tended to ignore little towns like Florence, South Carolina, or Eden Prairie, Minnesota. That's because there's not enough business in such places to support one of their high-priced salespeople.

"Initially we did just what everybody else did," he says. "We went to the big cities first. But we had people from Fargo and Muncie and Missoula and Sioux Falls and Des Moines and places like that saying, 'Can we handle your product?' So then we looked at those markets and we said, 'Good grief! Muncie was selling just as much as Chicago was. Why is that?' And then we found out that when you went to Muncie there was only one other company there—IBM."

And what was Scheff doing in Muncie? "Since I was a former dealer, our strategy was to market through dealers. Just about everyone else went direct. As such, they didn't end up in the Muncies and the Des Moines and the East Molines and places like that. We did."

But how long would that niche last?

Scheff might well have fretted about IBM. There was no escaping the industry's great mass-marketer. But instead he figured the market would be educated and increased demand would be created. Says Scheff: "We used to tell all our dealers that they should have a chapel, and on the altar there should be two candles, a big one and a small one: the big one should be for IBM, and the little one for Xerox, because without all their efforts we'd probably be about a $5 million company today."

It worked for a while. In 1983 CPT ranked third in the word processor market, trailing only IBM and Wang. Its numbers were enviable: Net income of $1 million in 1976 reached $17.7 million in 1983. The stock, which traded at $.50 a share in 1976 reached $28.00, and a lofty twenty-six times earnings six years later.

But CPT is not in the railroad supply business, where market changes are glacial in pace. CPT is in the much faster paced data processing business. Before Dean Scheff knew what had happened, the big-city producers had outflanked his regional niche without even trying.

Stand-alone word processors were caught in a squeeze play between the personal computers at the low end of the market (there are already 3.5 million of them on office desks around the country) and by total office automation systems at the high end. Distribution patterns changed as the market grew, signaling the end of regional niches.

"The competition came to us, courtesy of the Computer-lands and the Businesslands and Sears, and you name it," says Scheff. "That wiped out our initial concept."

It was clear that CPT lacked the resources to compete in the high-volume, low-margin PC market. It was equally clear that low-priced PCs were stealing its market. CPT's prices and profit margins crumbled. In 1981 CPT's standard word processor sold for eighteen thousand dollars. Today you can buy one for one-third of that.

---

*A regional niche probably won't last long in a business in which technology is changing rapidly or in which the major markets have become saturated.*

---

Scheff sought refuge in his own sales doctrine. "Our response was that we're in this business because of IBM, not in spite of them, so our equipment is now completely compatible with the IBM PC. We can put our word processing onto their PC, or we can take a PC along with our system and network it into our small- and large-cluster system."

That change in strategy put quite a strain on Scheff's sales force, however. "Our distribution system has to learn the complexities of networking," he concedes. "I'm convinced that that's one of the problems that the industry has right now. Firms have gone out and bought a huge number of PCs and said, 'Go forth and be productive.' So now everybody has a PC on their desk. How come we're not more productive? Today we can bring the ability to cluster networks, transfer files. To give you an example, we went into a university not too long ago, and the president had an Apple, a Macintosh, which he thought was the most fantastic thing he's ever used in his life. Two of his assistants had IBM PCs, which they thought were fantastic. And two of their secretaries had CPTs, which they thought were fantastic. Well, we're one of the few companies in the world that can take those three pieces of equipment and network them together."

Wouldn't it be logical to assume that IBM could do the same? "Oh, IBM has been doing that all along," says Scheff.

In other words, Scheff is fighting back the only way he can. He is offering customers IBM and Wang-compatible software to protect his hardware. But obviously this is forcing him to compete head-to-head with IBM and Wang, and thus to abandon his basic strategy. So now he is looking for new niches—market pockets like computers specifically designed for architects and engineers, both of whom need to manipulate flat-plane graphics, text, and numbers within the same document. Another market that interests him is high-volume text and form processors for the legal market.

To his credit, Scheff has moved quickly. CPT was first on the market with a hookup to the Westlaw database for lawyers. Trouble is, Prime and Apollo are already in the architect and engineer markets, and Wang, IBM, and Lanier in the text processor market.

Earnings are suffering. "Nineteen eighty-five was the first loss year in fifteen," says Scheff. "There's a variety of humble people around here all working much harder than they did in the past."

What has Scheff learned from this? "I think one of our primary mistakes was not exploiting advertising the way our friends at Apple did," he replies. Whether that could have protected a purely geographical niche in a rapidly growing market is highly debatable, however. To any customer, the more compatible the home and office computers are nationwide the better. And the more technologically advanced they are the better. That would seem to give a significant advantage to the larger and wealthier producers, but Scheff is not ready to acknowledge that. Niches will still exist in data processing, he believes. He just picked the wrong one: "The typing area in which we made our niche has indeed become a commodity market."

"We got complacent," he goes on. "It's difficult not to when you're growing fifty to 60 percent a year. It's awfully difficult to look inward and say, 'Gee, we must be doing something wrong.' If someone suggests you're getting complacent, the first thing you want to do is poke the guy in the chops. But when that growth tapers off, and you get a chance to look backward and reflect a little bit, you say, 'Hmm, maybe we were complacent!' "

# 19

## Crumbs from the Table

Crawford & Co. of Atlanta, Georgia, looks as though it has a niche that must be as safe as one could imagine. Over the past decade, for example, only in recession year 1981 did the company even show a modest dip in earnings, as revenues more than tripled from $54 million.

True, return on equity has dipped from a spectacular 27 percent to a merely outstanding 22 percent in recent years on virtually no debt, but that is at least partly attributable to the costs of branching out successfully into related fields.

How does Crawford do it? Crawford specializes in the nasty business of insurance claims adjusting—mainly involving auto accidents and workmen's compensation. It is the only public company in the field, running neck and neck in size with the privately held General Adjustment Bureau. Crawford takes the cases its insurance company clients don't have time for. "They'd rather do it themselves," says Crawford Chairman T. Gordy Germany. "But for lots of reasons they find that they're not able to do it as it should be done. You can't just put a claim on the edge of the desk and wait until somebody happens to get free to handle it. People expect when they call their agent or their insurance company that something is going to happen! Particularly if it's a crisis where somebody's injured, or your house is on fire."

Crawford, in other words, has found a niche taking care of the industry leftovers, competing mainly with individual claims adjusters for those crumbs. As long as the main market is growing, and as long as the competition for the leftovers remains highly fragmented, that can be very lucrative, as Don Brinckman at Safety Kleen discovered.

Crawford & Co. is able to offset the industry's modest cyclicity to some extent by being a nationwide company. "If you have the geographical spread that we do," Germany says, "it will balance out."

Even the recent prolonged downturn in the property and casualty insurance business didn't hurt Crawford particularly. "An insurance company won't necessarily refer out more or fewer claims just because they're financially flush or are having underwriting losses," he explains. "The claims that come in have to be handled. They can't say, 'Gee, we can't handle it this week because we've got a little underwriting loss problem here.' Somebody's got to handle that claim whether the insurer is rolling along or not."

It's not what you'd call a congenial business. Crawford field people, all college graduates, are not exactly greeted with open arms by accident victims worried about being able to pay the hospital bills. Besides, the pay is low. So Crawford's staff turnover is quite high.

---

*Sometimes the sheer unpleasantness of the work offers the protection of a niche if you develop systems to cope with it more efficiently than most.*

---

Furthermore, Crawford is highly vulnerable to process changes in his market since there's not a single thing Crawford does that its insurance company clients can't do just as well. Today, for example, Crawford's clients are handling an ever-increasing number of claims by telephone. Arguably that is one logical result of the market simplification introduced by no-fault auto insurance. But the trend clearly cuts down the volume of Crawford's traditional in-person auto claims adjusting business.

So Crawford has diversified into such related fields as claims adjusting for the growing number of self-insured corporations, for property insurers, and for medical benefit insurers. More imaginatively, Crawford has also moved into the rehabilitation services that many states require insurance companies to provide for people with long-term disabilities.

"I don't think there's much finesse to our marketing," says Germany. "It's just service."

# 20

## The Shrinking Pond Gambit

Bill O'Neill of International Clinical Laboratories in Nashville, Tennessee, has also struck it rich doing an industry's dirty work. But it didn't start out that way.

Time was when running a clinical testing laboratory for doctors and hospitals used to be a money machine. There were no restraints on doctors or hospitals as to how much testing they could do. Why should there be? The patient's insurance would cover it. For the independent laboratory the economies of scale were obvious: Testing equipment is expensive, so the more hours in the day it's used, the lower the cost of each analysis. Smaller hospitals and even some larger ones found independent test laboratories quite economical.

The field was soon crowded—often by doctors with an entrepreneurial flair and an interest in tax shelters. But as medical costs skyrocketed, insurance companies started pressuring hospitals to cut costs. That was bad news for the labs. Over the past ten years over half of the fifteen thousand medical test laboratories in the country went under.

Then came the coup de grâce. In an attempt to slap on a top limit on reimbursement and curb abuses, the Federal government standardized the care it regarded as appropriate for any given diagnosis financed by Medicare. They called it DRG—Diagnosis-Related Groups. Hospitals treating Medicare patients that offered more care than that prescribed under DRG—including additional laboratory testing—would simply not be paid for that care. Blue Cross/Blue Shield and other private insurers soon followed suit. Laboratory testing services became a fast-shrinking pond.

But you can be the biggest frog in a shrinking pond if you know that pond really, really well, as Bill O'Neill does. All you have to do is be the most cost-efficient player in the industry and let your customers know about it.

Bringing business common sense to the mom-and-doc lab business was O'Neill's entrepreneurial vision from the start. He got into it when its future looked limitless. Back in 1970 right after the height of the conglomerate craze, he and his second-in-command Mike Jeub were recruited to a new, fast-growing laboratory testing company that had just made over thirty acquisitions in a little over a year. Its customers were mainly doctors, not hospitals. Jeub was a former senior partner with Big Eight accounting firm Ernst & Whinney, and O'Neill, a Harvard Business School graduate, had been a division manager for an eye-care company in Fort Worth.

Both realized very quickly that, exciting as the marketing aspects of the business may have been, they had made a disastrous career choice. The company had virtually no controls and no strategy. Jeub had the courage to say so in a meeting. O'Neill backed him up from the operating viewpoint. The chief executive, who probably knew he was already in hot water, encouraged them to correct the problems. As they set about doing that, the chief executive was fired.

So O'Neill and Jeub tried to make sense out of chaos. First they defined the business. It seemed to have a wholesale side and a retail side. That in turn suggested two different pricing structures. It was the most fundamental kind of marketing analysis there is.

And then they asked, What equipment did it take to set up the most rudimentary regional office? How much business justified expansion of that office's plant and equipment?

They were also basic questions, but ones that had been ignored by most of the industry. Up until then the business had just been growing so fast that such common business sense hardly mattered.

---

*A specialist may be entrepreneur enough to spot an opportunity, but then overlook the basics—such as pricing structures.*

---

There was little O'Neill and Jeub could do about the debt load the company was carrying from its acquisition binge, however. As price cutting swept the industry (thanks to cost containment efforts and increased competition), they were forced to sell off assets to cover interest payments. Noting their vulnerability, and yet aware of their competence, a privately held string of laboratories named International Clinical Laboratories run by doctors proposed merger in the midseventies. The doctors wanted O'Neill and Jeub to manage the combine, using the ICL name. O'Neill and Jeub accepted, having little to lose. After all, it would get them into the hospital lab management business, which was far less competitive—being larger in scale—than servicing individual doctors.

At ICL all of O'Neill and Jeub's painstaking analysis began to pay off. While larger competitors began selling out to such consumer marketing giants as Hoffman La Roche (Biomedical Reference Laboratories), Corning Glass (Metpath), Revlon (National Health Laboratories), and American Hospital Supply (Bio Science), International Clinical Laboratories ranked near the top of the industry in profitability with a 16 percent return on equity and a low one-to-five debt-equity ratio.

Not long ago they convinced large voluntary hospitals to let ICL manage their laboratories in cost-saving joint ventures. Recently, ICL stock has been selling at nearly twice the average price-earnings multiple in the market because its earnings record had proved so reliable—despite the carnage in the rest of the industry.

# 21

## The Shotgun Solution

In some big consumer market industries you only find a niche, say some entrepreneurs, by constant innovation. The trouble is those innovations will be instantly copied by the big manufacturers. In short, it's a game for high rollers.

Take Minnetonka, for example. Nobody ever said Minnetonka chairman Bob Taylor wasn't innovative or that he lacked guts. What unbiased observers might say, however, is that Taylor tends to underestimate his far larger competitors such as Procter & Gamble and Colgate.

At twenty-six, shortly after leaving a promising career as a salesman for Johnson & Johnson, Taylor decided to make hand-rolled soap for gift shops. The gift shops were buying such soap from Europe and paying handsome premiums for it. Surely they would rather have a less expensive, and perhaps more reliable, local producer.

It was not exactly what you'd call an earth-shaking marketing insight. It wasn't even a very practical idea, said some. The method for producing the soap was obsolete. So Taylor hit the local library, figuring if his grandmother could make cold-process soap, then so could he. And he did. Trouble was, Taylor didn't have the cash to build a plant to make it in any volume.

But necessity is the mother of invention. On the theory that misery might like some company, Taylor found his way to Waterloo, Iowa, where Rath Packing was losing money carcass after carcass. Meatpackers like Rath produce tallow as a by-product. Tallow is the key ingredient in soap. Taylor offered to buy that tallow at a premium price if Rath would cook it into soap for him. Rath was desperate, and Taylor was in business.

Ever the pragmatist, Taylor even found an obsolete sausage-casing machine that could take the sixty-pound blocks Rath was cranking out and extrude it into sausage-sized lumps suitable for hand-rolling.

Pretty soon Taylor was flooding the gift shops with his Village Bath line of inexpensive soap specialties. Upgrading, he acquired Claire Burke, a fragrance producer dealing in perfumes and potpourri (dried petals and spices kept in a jar for their aroma). Then he entered a bigger distribution channel. He hired sales representatives to get into department stores.

By 1972, having more than doubled his sales volume every year for nine years, he started to sell his stock nationally. Pretty soon Minnetonka common was trading at forty times earnings.

At this point, smitten by the desire for large numbers, Taylor decided Minnetonka could be a major corporation as big as Procter & Gamble. So he started to act as though it were.

Specifically, he started to copy their ideas—a significant departure from his prior strategy. Taylor tried to copy Mary Kay and Avon with a direct-sales approach based in drugstores called "Milkmaid." Instead of giving Tupperware parties or calling door to door, Taylor's Milkmaids accosted drugstore customers with handsomely packaged cosmetics products. The Milkmaid program soon went sour.

Then Taylor bought Miraq, a company with a product he thought could give American Home Products' Woolite a run for its money. Miraq went quickly down the drain.

Meanwhile Gillette and Clairol had noticed and copied Taylor's Village Bath line. Taylor was in trouble. By 1974 Minnetonka shares were trading between ⅛ and ⅜. Minnetonka had lost half the equity it had just three years before.

But Taylor dug in his heels. He rebuilt that equity by paying attention to his existing lines and not indulging in daring new product launches. But four years later Taylor was back at it again, test-marketing a pump-dispensed liquid soap called Softsoap. None of the big soap companies could possibly copy him, he reasoned, because to do so would be to demonstrate the liabilities of their top-selling bar soaps. Used bar soaps were a sticky, unsightly mess, whereas Softsoap was a tidy little bottle. Taylor used traditional food brokers this time to get his product right up there on the supermarket shelves beside P&G and Colgate. He bet the company on Softsoap, spending $6 million on the nationwide launch.

For a while it looked as if Taylor had really done it. The product got off to a fast start, and earnings nearly quadrupled to $5.5 million in 1980. Anyone who had bought Minnetonka stock early that year could have made ten times his money in months, as the stock went from 1⅝ to 16⅜.

But Softsoap's heavy promotion allowed competitors like Jergens simply to introduce copies without advertising and undercut Taylor's price. Other me-toos soon swamped the market and Minnetonka with it. One year later in 1981, Minnetonka shares were back down around 3⅞, as earnings sank to $1.2 million and then into the red.

What was Taylor's response? In 1984 he launched a new product called Check Up, a pump-dispensed toothpaste. There was a difference this time, however. This time it was someone else's new product, launched in part with that someone else's money. And the someone else: West Germany's $3.3 billion chemical and consumer products giant Henkel, which had staying power.

Once again the early numbers are encouraging. But Colgate and others are already marketing a me-too product priced substantially below Check Up. Says Taylor: "I feel good. My opponents have practiced bulldozer marketing on me, but I have been surviving the onslaught of the giants. Now we've reached a critical mass. Now we can compete with them on more than one product."

---

*To break out of a specialty distribution niche and go head-to-head with the nationwide consumer goods companies, you need a giant ally as well as a superior product.*

---

What has been happening to Bob Taylor can happen to anyone with a good idea for a consumer product that isn't too costly or technically difficult to make. It may have taken former shopping center developer Vincent Marotta three long years to come up with his Mr. Coffee machine, but soon after the inevitable knockoffs began to appear from the likes of Norelco and General Electric. After the Cuisinart food processor hit the department stores, the Hamilton Beach division of Scovil was marketing one of the first knockoffs at half of Cuisinart's retail price. It is hard to topple a consumer giant.

# 22
## Sharpshooting

It's a fact that markets dominated by far larger competitors tend to stay dominated by the giants. According to a study done by marketing consultants Lubliner-Saltz Inc., the leading brand over sixty years ago is still the leading brand today in sixteen of eighteen major consumer products:

| Product | 1923 | 1984 |
|---|---|---|
| Bacon | Swift | First |
| Cameras | Kodak | First |
| Canned fruit | Del Monte | First |
| Canned milk | Carnation | First |
| Chewing gum | Wrigley | First |
| Chocolates | Hershey | Second |
| Flour | Gold Medal | First |
| Mint candies | Life Savers | First |
| Paint | Sherwin Williams | First |
| Pipe tobacco | Prince Albert | First |
| Razors | Gillette | First |
| Sewing machines | Singer | First |
| Soap | Ivory | First |
| Soft drinks | Coca-Cola | First |
| Soup | Campbell | First |
| Tea | Lipton | First |
| Tires | Goodyear | First |
| Toothpaste | Colgate | Second |

Source: Lubliner-Saltz Inc.

Nonetheless there is a more successful variation on the Bob Taylor shotgun approach to such markets. Instead of attacking everywhere, aim carefully at where your far larger competitors may be weakest. Then invest as much capital and manpower as you can.

Molex competes head-to-head in electrical connectors against a longtime Wall Street favorite called AMP, of Harrisburg, Pennsylvania. AMP is about ten times the size of Molex. There's also Burndy, another well-managed company that's twice Molex's size. But year after year both AMP and Burndy, good as they are, take a back seat to Molex in profitability. For the past ten years Molex has averaged a return on stockholder equity of 31 percent. In 1984 Molex showed a return on equity of 27.7 percent. Earnings have grown steadily over the decade—50 percent a year in good times, perhaps 10 percent in bad—from $2.4 million to $38.2 million as sales went from just $26 million to $252 million. The stock, despite four splits, has gone from five to forty-two in the past six years with scarcely a pause, yet recently it sold for just fifteen times earnings— only modestly above market averages.

In part that may be due to the fact that the founding Khrebiel family owns nearly half of the stock—which, as a consequence, is hard to get and therefore not as actively traded. The relative cheapness of the stock may also be due to the fact that the company is so well protected against takeover in a market that has been preoccupied with the fast profits of takeovers.

How does Molex manage to be far more profitable year after year than its far larger, well-managed competitors? By never varying from the hugely successful strategy laid down back in the fifties by Chairman and cofounder John H. Khrebiel.

That strategy in a nutshell: pick your product line very carefully and then give it everything you've got. In a fragmented marketplace where AMP, for example, might have nearly two hundred product lines, Molex would have fewer than twenty. In other words, Khrebiel tries to be as big a factor in the markets he does enter as AMP. And he doesn't enter a market unless he's sure there's enough business there and that Molex has enough of a competitive edge in design to justify tooling up for it. Then he prices the product to guarantee the kind of returns he wants and moves into the market aggressively.

What Khrebiel will not do is buy his way into a market. Any job shop—or "alley shop," as Khrebiel refers to them—can do that. Entering a market just because he can still make a profit at a significantly lower price is something he says he never does. If he did, the leading producer could always force him to discount still further until his profit margins were at commodity levels.

---

*Keep looking for those limited markets where you have a genuine competitive edge. That's where profitability and security lie. Tempting as it may be, don't try to buy your way into markets where you offer the same product at a lower price. That's where you'll be vulnerable.*

---

Khrebiel also will not do business with a contractor—like the U.S. military—that is too well funded to have to worry about choosing low-cost suppliers. If the customer has no appreciation of the value in dealing with Molex, Khrebiel doesn't want its business. It would sap his company's critical advantage—its discipline.

There have been mistakes. Molex tried and failed to service the hand-held calculator market and the video game market. But those were the exceptions.

Khrebiel learned his discipline young. Molex was once an alley shop, for many years after he and his brother started it in 1938. Scars of the depression are still there. Khrebiel says he will never borrow for working capital, no matter how good the opportunity. In overborrowed America, those words are almost painful to hear—because they are so embarrassingly sensible.

It was in the alley shop days also that Khrebiel learned the value of proprietary products. The minute Molex got any working capital to call its own from doing custom job shopwork, Khrebiel and his designers would set to work trying to come up with a proprietary product. It was a propitious time, of course. The postwar market was booming, and electrical appliances were just coming into their own, to be followed by the electronic era. So there were plenty of new opportunities about. But notice that Khrebiel didn't get caught the way John Grove of JLG did by spreading himself too thin. He refused to expand faster than his cash on hand.

From the beginning Khrebiel was totally market-oriented. Quickly he learned that what manufacturers of electrical consumer products wanted was ease of installation. Obvious as that may seem, it's the kind of thing an engineer tends to lose sight of in all the swirl of detail on a blueprint. So ease of installation became his design guideline.

Mighty Western Electric, as it used to be called, was brilliantly outflanked by Sweden's L. M. Ericsson in the late seventies when Ericsson came up with a totally modular telephone switching system that eliminated the need for highly trained personnel in remote locations. If part sixty-seven failed, a light would go off, and a worker could simply reach for another part sixty-seven to replace it. Such ease of operation and replacement is particularly valuable in a developing country with a scarcity of well-educated technicians. Of course, designing a modular switching device takes a totally different philosophical approach to engineering than Western Electric was used to in the United States, where there was always a highly trained team of

Bell technicians available for service calls. You can't do that in Saudi Arabia or Indonesia—and the market for telephone equipment, as Ericsson well knew, was now in the developing world.

Why did Ericsson come up with that and not Western Electric? For the same reason that Molex is doing so well: Ericsson comes from a small country, so some 90 percent of its sales have traditionally been to the export market. Maybe that makes Ericsson salespeople listen to the market needs more carefully.

It is that same hunger at Molex that makes Khrebiel give himself a tiny office that many top corporate trainees would feel rather insulted to be given. You don't miss the point: This is a no-frills organization. Everything is spent on the product, very little for the ego of the worker.

When Khrebiel has been earning close to 30 percent on shareholder equity for at least the past decade, it's hard to argue with his results.

# 23

## Keys to Successful Marketing

Entrepreneurial marketing is like guerilla warfare. First you find a protected enclave from which you can launch your first small attacks without worrying about being overrun by far larger competition. Then you build, looking for chinks in Goliath's armor.

Like guerilla leaders, you are frequently distracted from the strategic questions because you are amassing an army at the same time. And you may not have many talented lieutenants, or even sergeants, to help you.

That's why when you ask any veteran entrepreneur what marketing advice he'd offer to another businessman just starting his own company, he'll generally tell you what he overlooked or underestimated—and then what he learned from his mistakes.

After all, there are many more opportunities for mistakes than there are opportunities for triumph for either an entrepreneur or a guerilla leader. And the consequences of error can be grave indeed. The only way to learn is to observe the many styles of entrepreneurial marketing that have gone before.

Think of tiny Brenco watching Timken's railroad roller bearings come on the market and realizing not only that an alternate supplier could survive but that there would be time to finance and build up a competitive manufacturing base in easy stages. That's an insight that no rookie in the business could probably have managed.

But often the business the entrepreneur is entering doesn't exist. So the entrepreneur has to make all the early mistakes himself. Think of the marketing hurdles that U.S. Surgical had to leap before hitting it big in surgical staplers with a highly specialized, extremely costly approach that Hirsch would probably have thought insane at the outset. And think also of the staying power—both financial and emotional—that that required.

In franchising, LeVine of Postal Instant Press had to learn it all from scratch. On the other hand, someone like Perry Mendel of Kinder-Care Learning Centers, a veteran real estate developer, knew most of the ins and outs of capital-intensive franchising early on.

Former stockbroker John Folkerth of Shopsmith probably skimmed his market for home woodworking tools out of inexperience in the field, whereas Twentieth Century Insurance's Lou Foster, with experience in a huge market, did not.

But industry experience isn't everything. Hack Miller of Rival Manufacturing with his Crockpot, John Grove of JLG with his construction equipment, and Dean Scheff of CPT with his word processors were all veterans in their businesses and fell into the skimming trap just the same. So, one might argue, did Matty Simmons of National Lampoon, whose particular brand of humor may have peaked with its generation.

Just recognizing a niche can be extraordinarily difficult, even if it's sitting right in your own backyard. Warren Musser of Safeguard Industries, as it used to be called, was as knowledgeable as anyone could wish about the value of market niches. Top investment bankers were on his board of directors. And yet it took years for him to realize that a little accounting notebook company he'd acquired years ago was his crown jewel.

Doing an industry's dirty work is an entrepreneurial gambit that has worked over and over again. T. Gordy Germany of Crawford & Co. in claims adjusting, Don Brinckman of Safety Kleen in service station and restaurant parts cleaning, and Mike Jeub of International Clinical Labs in hospital lab testing have all taken that route. Trouble is, that's a fairly obvious type of niche. So there is generally lots of competition. As a result, the winner is usually the one who can understand and systematize the business the best.

Or contrast the incredibly different strategies of the Khrebiels of Molex with their rifle-shot approach to the electrical connector business with the shotgun approach to the soap business of Minnetonka's Bob Taylor. Who is right? That is difficult to say. If yours is a business of hundreds and thousands of small products for very specific needs like Molex's, then concentration on technical advantage is the key to marketing success. But if yours is a mass market like consumer soaps, then there may be no innovation you can make that the competition cannot me-too off the shelves unless you have an equally powerful ally.

The first questions any general will ask himself in mapping strategy have always been about enemy strength and type of terrain. The answers to those questions can dictate vastly different strategies. If yours is the comparatively level battlefield, then a massive armored assault may be the best—if you can match the forces of the opposition. Light, highly mobile infantry may be better if you find yourselves in the swampy lowlands.

Some knowledge of the history of your business can help you enormously. Germany's brilliant armored commander Erwin Rommel was a close student of the cavalry movements in the American Civil War. His American counterpart, General George Patton, was an avid student of classical military history. If studying the foraging and harassing sweeps of Jeb Stewart's Confederate cavalry, the strategic genius of Stonewall Jackson, or the tactics of the Spartan stand at Thermopylae gave those generals invaluable insights, it probably follows that studying the marketing tactics, successes, and failures of other entrepreneurs makes great sense for those who want to start their own business. That history can serve both as a source of new ideas and as a warning about or confirmation of strategies you are contemplating.

# Part III
# MANAGEMENT

# 24

## The Way You Go about Making Money Runs Contrary to What Got You into Business in the First Place

A true story: When one of the coauthors was fifteen, he accompanied his father to shop for a new car. The plan of attack was simple. There were four Plymouth dealers within ten miles of their house, and father and son would visit all four, shop for the best price, and turn over the down payment.

Three of the car salesmen were nondescript and didn't appear to be overly interested in selling a car on that rainy Saturday afternoon. Each offered a price within fifty dollars of the others.

But the fourth man made a lasting impression. It wasn't his appearance. Dewey looked the same as all the others in his sportscoat and mismatched pants. What lingered was what he said.

It happened after the dickering ended over the price of the Plymouth (a gold Fury III with a black vinyl roof would be the car the coauthor would borrow for high school dates).

"How can you sell this car for $150 less than everyone else?" Dewey was asked as he drew up the papers.

"Well," said Dewey seriously after pulling on his cigarette, "we lose money on every sale but make it up in volume."

## Funny but True

Getting a money-making idea is one thing. Making money from it is quite another. The salesman's wry comment on losing money on every sale but making it up in volume is amusing, but all too true for many entrepreneurs. After getting a good idea and finding a market, they suddenly discover they are losing money on each sale and continue to do so until they go out of business. The joke turns out to be on them.

The third phase in a small company's life cycle—the part in which it should start making money—is when an entrepreneur discovers if he has the resourcefulness to turn an ethereal idea into a solid reality. Getting most ideas to the profit-making stage takes more work than you might expect. The hard part is not, as we have seen, coming up with a blockbuster idea—the concept doesn't have to be terrific. *Implementing* an idea is where the entrepreneur often stumbles on the road to riches. Implementation requires attention to details that may seem obvious when viewed with hindsight but aren't at the time.

That puzzled us for a long time. Why do many entrepreneurs have problems dealing with growth? About half of the companies that pass the financial screens to qualify as one of the best small companies in America one year will fail to repeat the next. Why?

It turns out that dealing with growth hurdles almost always requires the entrepreneur to think in ways that are *the exact opposite* of what initially made him a success. Why this is so becomes clear if you trace the route that all entrepreneurs take.

In the beginning there is the idea. It comes from the entrepreneur. He thought of it, and only he, at first, understands it. From there the entrepreneur works to build a company. At first, he makes all the decisions himself and does almost all the work—from product design to bookkeeping—alone. Most often he doesn't have any choice. There is simply no money to pay anyone else.

But that very self-reliance, which is vital to getting the company up and running, can keep it from growing later. "I built this company; I am responsible for making it what it is today, and only *I* can know what is best for its future," is an attitude common in people who start companies.

---

*Your company doesn't have to do everything itself. Let suppliers do what they are best at, and concentrate on the original part of your idea.*

---

That independence to the point of orneriness is fine when a company is small. One of the great advantages an emerging growth company enjoys is its lack of structure. There is no bureaucracy to keep it from exploiting openings in the marketplace.

But the desire for complete control—expressed consciously as when the owner/founder says, "Only I know," or subconsciously (as through the entrepreneur's inability to delegate authority, hire strong people, or plan for an orderly succession) is a major problem. It limits growth.

Quite simply, an entrepreneur can't do everything himself. And he shouldn't. But as we shall see, that lesson is difficult to learn.

# 25

## "You Have to Spend Money to Make Money," and Other Lies

An entrepreneur searching for a role model shouldn't look to Ray Kroc, who spotted the potential in the McDonald brothers' hamburger stand, or to Henry Ford. He should look at the antithesis of individuality—the International Business Machine Corp. (IBM).

Specifically, he should look at the way IBM created its personal computer (PC). As everyone knows, IBM didn't invent the personal computer. The prototype for the industry, the Altair, appeared in the mid-1970s. Apple Computer revolutionized the marketplace with the Apple II a little later, and by the time IBM decided to enter the market, there were already dozens of small firms making personal computers.

But as we've already seen, entrepreneurship doesn't have to—and probably shouldn't—come from new ideas, and clearly the IBM PC was nothing new. What IBM did when it decided to go into the personal computer business in 1980 was very similar to what you do every Saturday morning. It went shopping.

If you take the PC apart, you'll find dozens of separate components. Few were made by IBM. The $45 billion company simply scoured the country, buying disk drives from

Tandon in Chatsworth, California, software from Microsoft in Bellevue, Washington, and so forth. "Anybody could have done what we did," says an IBM spokesman candidly. "Part of the reason was speed. We wanted to enter the marketplace in a hurry, and it was quicker to buy off the shelf than it was for us to make it. The other reason was there was no compelling reason for us to do it ourselves. There were good components out there."

Think about that for a minute. Here is one of the most successful companies in American history saying, in essence, it didn't have to reinvent the wheel. There were good parts already out there; all we had to do was put them together. *"We didn't have to do everything ourselves."*

Put in italics, the statement looks so obvious as to be absurd. Yet if you look at the thousands of small companies that fail each year, you'll find there is at least one common thread: They spent money needlessly. Yes, if you are going to be in business, you have to produce a product. But that doesn't mean you have to manufacture it. Yes, your product will have to be packaged in something, but you don't have to package it.

Simply put, you don't have to spend money to make money. In fact, you shouldn't. Perhaps the best example of this is Marcia Tripp, president of Pawprints, a greeting card company in Jaffrey, New Hampshire.

## "I Would Be Nuts to Own a Printing Press"

It is more than the four hundred miles between Jaffrey, New Hampshire, and Armonk, New York, that separates Pawprints from IBM. While IBM produces sales of $45 billion and earnings of $6.5 billion, Pawprints records one one-thousandth of that. And while IBM believes its tens of thousands of employees throughout the world should work in teams and make group decisions, the thirty people who work at the greeting card company in southeastern New Hampshire exhibit the flinty independence associated with the Granite State.

Then there are the differences in what the companies make. For every circuit board and disk drive in an IBM computer, there is an anthropomorphic critter on a Pawprints greeting card. (A human-looking mouse hugging an olive with the inside caption reading 'Olive you' is Pawprints's version of the IBM PC—a runaway best-seller.)

Yet for all their differences, there are two important similarities: Both Pawprints and IBM have net profit margins that are about three times the averages reported by their competitors. And Pawprints makes its cards in the same way that IBM goes about assembling a PC; it farms out as much of the work as possible.

The way Marcy Tripp, forty, president of Pawprints, sums up her success as she sits in her small, cluttered office, is not all that different from the explanation you'll receive from top management at IBM's sprawling headquarters in Armonk: "You find people to help you provide the highest-quality product in the least expensive way. Then you get efficient."

That quest for efficiency, which has produced 15 percent net margins at Pawprints, has led Tripp to follow a path that some might find unusual. She has no staff artists for her greeting cards. The drawings are all done by free-lancers paid by the card. Tripp never sees the tons of paper Pawprints consumes each year—it is bought for her by an independent agent and shipped directly to the one of five printers she uses. She owns no printing presses, although they are the most important part of Pawprints's production.

"You need a one-million-dollar press to produce the quality printing on our cards," says Tripp. "Anyone who buys a press in this business is nuts. And they will go broke before they cart them away to the asylum."

The decision to contract for as much work as possible, which allows Tripp to do $8 million worth of sales annually with just thirty salaried employees, stems from Tripp's understanding of business. "There are only three ways to sell a product," she says. "You can import something and sell it. You can make something and sell it. Or you can publish."

Tripp has decided that Pawprints is a publisher—the writing and printing of its cards are done for it by others. But that simple explanation is more vital than you might think.

Tripp could have defined her company as a *producer and manufacturer* of artwork. If she had, staff artists would have been hired, a purchasing department would have been created, and printing presses would be found in the basement of her red barnlike building on Route 202 in Jaffrey. Had she believed the adage "You have to spend money to make money," Tripp would have been heavily into debt before she ever turned out her first card. And given the high overhead she would have created and her relatively small sales, Pawprints would have quickly gone bankrupt.

But while brilliant in retrospect, the decision to approach her business as a publisher was not planned. But then again, neither was the decision to go into business in the first place. "We didn't have any choice," says Tripp, who majored in English at the University of New Hampshire but never graduated. "We were broke."

"Wally [Marcy's husband, Wallace Tripp, author of such children's books as *Granfa Grig had a Pig; A Great Big Ugly Man Came Up and Tied His Horse to Me*] was doing children's books filled with nonsense rhymes. At that time you got a flat fee of five hundred dollars a book. If you killed yourself you could do six books a year. So at best, you'd make $3,000.

"To make some money we did drawings in black and white, because we couldn't afford color, and we had them printed on cards in Peterborough [the town next door to Jaffrey] and sold them to local stores," Marcy recalls.

A local card company noticed the Tripps' work and signed Wally to do cards for them. "We did it under a royalty arrangement, and they were an instant success," Marcy says. "But after two years the owner decided now that he was making money he wouldn't pay us. He just refused to pay us the royalties. So we went to Wally's parents—his father was an engineer who had some money—and said we'd like to go into business ourselves. Wally's parents put up the money and handled the books, and we did the creative part.

"Five years later, in 1976, we bought the company from my in-laws, and after four hours of instruction in business from my father-in-law, we took it over," Tripp says. "Our first card is still in the line. It's a turtle with a Band-Aid on his tummy with 'Get well soon' on the inside. We have made our money on simple, direct cards that are funny and witty. They are not complicated. The picture says most of it. The tag line, the inside caption, is obvious, but rewarding in its obviousness. People say, Ah, perfect! Of course!" Pawprints cards rely heavily on puns (a get-well card intended for someone who reads a lot has the caption "to my favorite ill literate") and feature clever drawings.

Tripp has given a lot of thought to what has made her company a success. "We are the classic case of finding our niche and sticking to it," she says. "We have a highly educated, upmarket clientele; people who can tell the difference between good drawing and bad drawing; people with wit. These are people who don't want everything said for them in sixteen lines or less.

"Greeting cards help people communicate with one another. On one hand, greeting cards insulate you from the receiver; you are saying, I am not going to hug you, but I am going to send you this card. And if it is a Pawprints card, it says, I know something special about you and show that I care enough to share something important with you.

"Sometimes it is a way to ease into a relationship," Tripp adds. "A few years ago, before it was okay for a woman to be aggressive, she would send a man our cards, and the indirect message was, I am bright and clever and you would like me if you knew me better."

Tripp's approach has worked well, and Pawprints seems destined for further success. It now sells its cards in the more than thirteen hundred Waldenbooks stores and is negotiating with other bookstore chains.

---

*Farming out as much work as you can means less money is tied up in production. But the biggest advantage is it gives an entrepreneur time. She isn't slowed down learning how to do something that a supplier is already expert at.*

---

But even as Pawprints's sales grow, Tripp has no thoughts of greatly expanding her work force or bringing more of the work inside in her plant. Why should I? she asks. "This is a very nice, neat, clean straightforward business. We are a publisher in the truest sense of the word. Our capital investment is small. Our inventory is small, and our receivables are excellent—they average forty-five days. Our net margins are 15 percent. Why would I want to change anything?"

The approach both Tripp and IBM use to produce their products has a lot to recommend it, even if it runs contrary to the entrepreneur's instinctive reaction to do everything himself.

Farming the work out means there is less money tied up in production. Some people assume that relying on outside suppliers costs much more than doing the job yourself. But if you have contractors compete for each job—for example, the five printers Tripp uses compete for each printing job—that higher cost is virtually eliminated.

But the biggest advantage in subcontracting is that it gives an entrepreneur time. He isn't slowed down learning how to do something that a supplier is already expert at.

What can be subcontracted? Breaking down a product to its basic parts—as we saw in chapter 4 of the "Idea" section—will suggest areas where the work can be farmed out. By figuring what components were needed to build the PC, IBM found dozens of places to subcontract. Tripp has found three: printing, the purchasing of the paper, and the artwork.

Contracting to have some of the basic work of the business done by others is not as alien as you might think. How many companies clean their own offices at night or have all their printing, legal, or accounting done internally?

The idea is to do a job as cheaply as possible. Sometimes it pays to have someone else do it.

# 26

## Details, Details, Details

With his feet up on the table in the conference room of his Fort Lauderdale office, Peter Halmos is Central Casting's idea of what the young head of an emerging growth company should look like. The forty-one-year-old executive is in shirtsleeves, tie askew, and sucking on a Popsicle. But if the image complete with Porsche parked right outside the door—is perfect for Hollywood, it fades fast when Halmos starts talking.

"I don't think I have accomplished anything, and I am frustrated as hell, and I grow more frustrated day by day."

At first blush, given what he has accomplished, that is hard to understand. His company consistently produces an average return on equity above 20 percent on no debt, and its stock consistently trades at a multiple of twenty times earnings. Halmos's achievements are of the sort other entrepreneurs envy, and given his company's beginnings, those results are even more impressive.

With his freshly minted M.B.A. from the University of Florida firmly in hand, Halmos went to work on Wall Street, in the fall of 1969, as a trainee in the investment trust department of the Bank of New York. It took him five months to realize he did not want to be an investment banker. He also realized, like most of the entrepreneurs who came before him, that he didn't want to spend the rest of his life working for someone else.

"I knew I wanted to do something on my own. But since I didn't have any money and didn't know how to get any, it had to be something simple to start," Halmos recalls. "So I started to think about services I could provide that were within my reach—and my reach extended to all of a hundred bucks."

But while he didn't have money, he did have two other things: a younger brother, Steve, who had just finished his M.B.A., and a lot of time—thanks to New York's dreary winters—to think about what kind of business he wanted to start.

"Steve and I liked the idea of doing something with the credit card industry, which was just getting a head of steam," Halmos says. "As more people got more cards, losing them would become a major problem. We also thought about the marketing potential. People with credit cards have similar demographics, so we would have a readily identifiable group to sell to. We also liked the idea of billing customers through their credit cards. It makes it easier to get customers to renew." Whatever service Halmos developed would run for a fixed time, say, one year. At the end of the year, the service would be automatically renewed, through a charge on the credit card statement. This is how the credit card companies themselves collect their annual fees.

"That was the key to the whole thing," Halmos adds. "We wanted to figure out something we could sell that would make money for us year after year after year. We didn't want to have to reinvent the wheel every year. This was the mold. We weren't really focusing on what the service would be. We didn't invent a mousetrap or try to create a product that would create a demand. We started in a way all the books tell you not to. We started by asking what kind of economic concept made sense and then asked what possible service would fit the concept. It was the cart before the horse."

From all these criteria sprang an idea that would become known as Hot Line, a form of insurance. For a fee of what is now fifteen dollars a year, a customer registers all his credit cards with SafeCard. Should the cards become lost or stolen, the customer makes one toll-free call to SafeCard, which notifies all the credit card companies and arranges for new cards to be sent.

"It sounded simple and sounded like a service everyone should have. It was just common sense," Halmos says. He is being too modest.

Consider what he did. He did not create a new concept. He took a proven idea—insurance—and applied it to a new area (as discussed in chapter 4 of the "Idea" section)—credit cards.

But Halmos even went further. He—like Marcy Tripp and the creators of the IBM PC—let other people do most of the work for him. Potential customers learn about Hot Line through a flier enclosed with their monthly credit card bill, not through a separate mailing from SafeCard. If they sign up, the annual charge appears on their credit card statement. They do not pay SafeCard. (SafeCard is paid by the credit card company, which keeps a part of the annual fee for its trouble.)

"All this was part of the mold," Halmos recalls. "For example, the cost of advertising is very high. When you don't have the money, you have to find a cheaper alternative. Getting something to ride along with the bill the credit card issuer sends to a customer is far less expensive than doing a separate mailing yourself."

The idea for the Hot Line protection service and the way Halmos went about setting up his company may look brilliant in retrospect, but his idea did not take the world by storm. It took Halmos six years to sign his first major credit card customer. The memories of those six years are not pleasant. "We suffered," Halmos says simply. "During my spare time I would find soda pop bottles and turn them in for money. There was lots of discouragement. Many times we were facing extinction." It was a matter of starting slow and then not going anywhere.

In SafeCard's early days, Halmos used an answering service to handle the phone calls from people who lost their credit cards. Then Halmos personally notified the credit card companies.

"Most of our time was spent just trying to raise money to stay alive," he recalls. "In 1971 we had a small public offering, which raised $250,000. Once we had some money we were able to design computer programs to handle the service. All the while, we kept calling on the credit card issuers, hoping they would let us market Hot Line through them."

Halmos also used the money from that tiny stock sale to acquire other small companies with similar ideas. Not only did that reduce competition, but these companies, which did their mailings through local banks and stores, had enough income to keep SafeCard going, while Halmos kept trying for those six years to land a national account. "We stayed alive, and that is about it" is how Halmos sums up SafeCard's history from 1969 to 1975.

"The thing that kept us going and kept my faith over all those years, when all my friends with jobs were getting raises and I couldn't even afford a beer, was the fact that we had worked out the economics in the first place. We knew the thing would work if we had the chance," Halmos says. "It wasn't a question of whether you make money or lose it, under the way we set it up. It was only a question of how soon you made money."

Halmos needed just one big customer to prove him right. In 1975, Atlantic Richfield decided to give Halmos's idea a try and offered his service to its three million credit card holders. The response was impressive, and Halmos never looked back. SafeCard now has more than 100 credit card companies—including American Express and the nation's major department store chains—as customers.

So why, now that SafeCard is a $40 million (revenues) company, is Pete Halmos frustrated?

He faces the problem that confronts the founder of every emerging growth company when it reaches SafeCard's point of development. Halmos describes the problem well: "It is very hard making the transition from doing it yourself to doing it through other people. That's probably the hardest thing there is."

---

*Expect to make 90 percent of your mistakes on people judgments.*

---

That transition is part of a larger, crucial change: the metamorphosis from being an entrepreneur to being an administrator. Halmos, who is handling the change better than most, still is having a hard time. "I would say we made nine-tenths of our mistakes on people and one-tenth on everything else. I can hardly think of any mistake we have made that didn't involve having the wrong person in the wrong place," he says. "My admiration for an effective manager has grown. I used to turn my nose up at them. But there really is a need for people with an ability to administer and manage. Getting things done through others is very hard."

But it has to be done. "If you are going to grow and do a good job, there comes a time when you can't follow up on all the details yourself," Halmos says.

As SafeCard became successful, that message hit Halmos in the face every day. He recalls a story that to him illustrates the problems he has had in changing from an entrepreneur to an administrator.

"It is Friday afternoon, and I am getting ready to go out

of town. A middle manager who works here has left me a couple of notes saying he has to see me, but I just haven't had the time, so he just shows up. He's in a jam. Unless he has seventeen thousand dollars by five P.M., he loses his house. Now, I just can't write him a check. The lawyer has to get involved. And I have to leave, so that means my brother Steve gets involved. And this guy's supervisor has to be called in. And before you know it, we've eaten up twenty to thirty hours of top management time over something that hasn't made us one dime. Now, multiply that by the number of people you have working here. They are not robots. They are people, and people have problems from time to time. But these kinds of things don't make us a dime. It has nothing to do with how many mailings go out and how many people are going to sign up for Hot Line."

## What's an Entrepreneur to Do?

By spending time on people problems, the entrepreneur/founder is kept away from the things he is good at—finding new markets, implementing new ideas. As a result his company suffers. It loses market share, or stops growing because the founder is forced to spend too much of his time looking inside his company, instead of searching outside for new markets. He is dealing with personal problems and the problems of managing growth that is coming faster than he ever dreamed of. As a result, he spends too little time doing what he should be doing: determining how to increase sales and profits.

It was while SafeCard suffered through these growing pains that it turned in its first year during which earnings did not top the preceding one.

Obviously the solution is to create layers of management that free the founder to think bigger thoughts than who should go on vacation when. But it is not that easy. Some entrepreneurs cannot give up control. They demand being involved in every detail. (Remember President Jimmy Carter's penchant for scheduling the use of the White House tennis court?) That is understandable. It was the entrepreneur's attention to detail that made him a success initially. However, that no longer works as his company succeeds.

But even when an entrepreneur like Halmos—who is willing to take the necessary step of giving up control—tries to delegate, he runs into problems.

"First of all, when you begin doing jobs through other people instead of doing them all yourself, you have a communication problem," he says. "What you say and what they hear are two different things. You have to be sure they do the job the way you think it should be done, and you have to make sure it gets done, period. Every time you add another layer, it is like playing telephone [the children's game in which a message is whispered in the ear of people sitting around in a circle]. By the time it gets back to you, it is an entirely different message."

In playing telephone, the more garbled the message becomes, the funnier the result. In the case of a small company, a garbled message can result in disaster.

"You find a head financial person," Halmos says, giving an example SafeCard lived through. "It takes a long time to get him acclimated. After you have talked to him about how the job should be done, he sets up a certain system of controls. He sets up that system while you are off doing other things. Later, you find out he did it wrong, and now you are worse off than if you hadn't done anything at all. You have a system, but it is the wrong one. You have to tear that down before you can build a correct one. When you are small and vulnerable one person can cause a lot of damage."

One way Halmos, like the heads of most emerging

growth companies, tried to increase his odds was by hiring executives from larger companies. Conventional wisdom holds that since these people have worked at companies that have grown successfully, they can impart what they have learned to companies just starting to grow.

The theory is fine. Reality is different. One frustrated chief executive at a $70 million high-tech company remembers his experience. "I was reprimanding one of our new people, an executive we had hired from IBM, for going over budget. He looked pained and said, 'How do you expect me to do my job? Don't you realize that I wasted more money at IBM in a week than you let me spend in a year?'"

The problem is executives from larger companies often cannot cope with the less structured, faster-paced environment they find at the small companies that hire them.

"We hired a very nice guy with good credentials and a fine record in a big company," Halmos recalls. "His work was solid, and the quality was good. There was only one problem. In this large company the amount of work one person does is a drop in the bucket compared to what one person does here. So before you know it you have a problem, and before you find out about it, you have a mess. And here is a fellow, a very fine guy, good intentions, but he just couldn't handle the job."

Handling problems such as these requires an entrepreneur like Halmos to become a manager. It isn't easy and often not desired. "There are some who can make the transition, and others who can't," Halmos says. "I know I can make it; I don't know if I want to."

Halmos is trying to solve that dilemma by going back to SafeCard's roots. He is using the same planning process that created the company to make it better. Formal systems for relaying information have been installed, and new managers with overlapping responsibilities have been hired. "Now if one person doesn't work out, the others can easily absorb what he was doing."

Those new SafeCard managers will be coming from outside the company. Halmos has realized a point that many
entrepreneurs are unable to grasp. The people who helped
get you started may not be the ones who can help you grow.
They may not have the ability, or be able to handle additional responsibility. In the long run, promoting them over
their heads will only hurt them—and the company.

"Our people are terrific and learning, but they are
young," Halmos says. "They need more seasoning. We are
searching for three people to fit between Steve and me. We
have our orchestra. We are looking for orchestra leaders.
We need people with gray hair. People who our people can
look up to."

---

*The people who helped you start a company may not have
the ability to help you grow it. Recognizing that fact and
realizing you have to bring in new people to help the company expand are two of the hardest things an entrepreneur
has to do.*

---

In the abstract, that sounds fine. However, when bringing in managers from the outside three things can happen,
and two of them are bad. It is possible that the new boss
will be treated with instant acceptance. Possible . . . but not
likely. The first reaction from people in the orchestra is
"Why shouldn't I lead the band?" Resentment is likely. So
are resignations from people you would prefer to keep.

The other problem is layers of management cut off the
employee from the leader. If you join IBM today, you don't
expect to waltz into the chairman's office any time you
choose. But at small companies, it is different. Employees
expect that kind of access. That is especially true of an employee who was there when the company was formed. He is
not going to like it when he finds the door to the boss's office is suddenly closed and he is told to see someone else—
someone with a less impressive title than CEO.

"For many people it is important to have access to the boss," Halmos has learned. "It says to them what they are doing is important, and the good ones see it as a way to learn. When they no longer have that access, you lose a lot of good people.

"But the boss can't do his job when he is spending all this time with these people," he adds. "That is why in our search for a new boss, or bosses, we waited until SafeCard could afford—both operationally and financially—to bring in managers whom others would view and accept as the boss.

"People do good work because they want to and can," Halmos adds. "When they don't do good work, it either means they can't or they don't want to. And to a great extent, it is the boss who determines whether they want to. But good managers just don't walk in off the street. They don't want to work for a small company. When you are $10 million to $15 million in revenues and asking where you are going, they are not going to come.

"We are now at the point where we can attract those people because we can offer them a challenge and a future," he says. "I think the company is strong enough now to go through a metamorphosis and become less of an extension of Steve and me."

The decision to bring in outsiders to manage SafeCard's growth is also a decision that Halmos thinks will be good for him.

"I have to make a choice. Do I stay an entrepreneur, or do I become a manager? I *know* I don't want to be a manager," Halmos says. "People excel when they get themselves in a position where they can take advantage of their strengths. Over the years, I have figured out where my aptitudes are, and they are not in managing an organization. I can do it, and if I really made my mind up, I think I could be pretty good at it. But for me to do it would be rubbing against the grain. I want to focus on the things that helped to get us where we are now. What is going to work? What isn't working? Why not? How do we fix it?

"When I interview people, I always ask them where they want to be five years from now," Halmos says. "I want to know what their goals are. If someone were to ask me that, I'd say that in five years I wouldn't want to be doing what I am doing now. It is not that I don't want to run SafeCard; it's just that I shouldn't be this involved in the day-to-day stuff. Fortunately, we are at the point where we can do something about it."

Halmos has realized that managing growth means putting in place systems so that the head of a small company can know what is going on from the information he receives, without having to be in the middle of everything every day. While sometimes there may be lags in the information the boss receives, those delays shouldn't be very long. Halmos puts it this way: "No disaster should be able to happen without me knowing about it. Nothing serious. Nothing fatal.

"I think I can do a lot if I am not involved with all the people and doing all the small administrative things that need to be done every day," Halmos adds. "A lot of people say, You have done fairly well, you should be proud of yourself. But it is all relative; it's like money. I used to think if I had the money I have now I wouldn't have to think about it; I'd have more than I could ever need. I don't feel that way. I feel broke.

"Your perceptions change if you're a person who is always striving."

## If It Is Broken, Fix It and Keep Fixing It

The problems and frustrations that Halmos encountered in creating SafeCard are not limited to start-ups. Ongoing operations have similar experiences—and woes. Consider Edward Botwinick's saga at Timeplex, about twelve hundred miles up the East Coast from SafeCard in Woodcliff Lake, New Jersey.

Timeplex was founded in 1969 by a group of engineers who had left Bell Labs and Western Union clutching a simple idea with a complicated name: time division multiplexing. That's a way of allowing a single phone line to be shared by many devices sending data at the same time. A multiplexer works similarly to an old-fashioned party line. The results of both are the same: a lower phone bill.

The concept behind the party line is simple: Since no person uses his phone twenty-four hours a day, it is possible for two or more people to share the same phone line. Time division multiplexing does the same thing for data devices that don't use the phone line's full capacity when they send information. It divides up the available capacity in the line, allowing two or more pieces of data to be sent at the same time—the key difference between a party line and multiplexing. With a party line, you have to wait until the other person is done using the line before you can take your turn. With a multiplexer, two or more messages can be sent at the same time.

The idea wasn't new. But up until Timeplex was started, the function of time division multiplexers was performed by large minicomputers programmed to multiplex, or divide up, the telephone line. The cost was fifty thousand to one hundred thousand dollars.

Timeplex took advantage of what was then a new generation of integrated circuits and produced a functionally equivalent device without the costly overhead baggage of a general-purpose computer. Timeplex's original multiplexers cost ten thousand to fifteen thousand dollars.

It was while the engineers were looking for funding for their idea that they met Botwinick.

Botwinick, whose speech is as blunt as his crewcut, understood what the engineers had. He has degrees in physics and engineering and was a founder of Silicon Transistor Corp. "After Silicon Transistor was sold in 1967, I wandered down to Wall Street by mistake—as an interim between jobs—and I ended up spending ten years there, doing venture capital and investment research in high tech," Botwinick says in typical machine-gun fashion. "Most of that time, I was vice-president in investment research for Goldman Sachs."

While at Goldman, Botwinick ran into the engineers who were trying to found Timeplex. "They were having trouble raising money because they had put together a rather specific, technical description of a product and a market that the financial community had no comprehension of.

"Their business plan was badly written and difficult to understand, and their presentation was very amateurish," he adds. "People who heard it said: 'I can't run this business—I don't have the technical understanding; and based on this business plan, I wouldn't trust these guys to run it.' I didn't disagree with that, but I felt given my interest and assistance I would be able to help them through a lot of problems."

Botwinick rewrote the business plan, reducing both its size—the final product was about six pages—and the engineers' sales and earnings forecasts, and took it to Goldman Sachs's board of directors. "The firm turned it down but gave me permission to do it on my own," he recalls about that meeting in 1969. "So I called a bunch of my friends and said, 'I am putting thirty thousand dollars of mine into this thing and I am trying to raise two hundred thousand dollars. Do you want to come along?' "

They did, and Botwinick joined Timeplex's board of directors. When the company went public in 1973, it had annual sales of $3 million. What followed, Botwinick says, is a classic form of deterioration.

"It was an engineering-based company where the engineers didn't feel it necessary or even appropriate to hire any business people," he says. "The company went broke for business reasons, not product reasons."

While on the board, Botwinick used his business connections to set up distribution and find clients, but he quickly felt unappreciated. "The guy who was running the company turned out to be quite an egotist," Botwinick says. "He did not want to take any advice or assistance from anyone. I resigned from the board when the company went public. I did not want the potential liability. I did not trust him or his ability."

By 1976 Timeplex's revenues were $6 million, but the company lost $450,000 for the year, after being forced by their auditors to take enormous asset write-downs, Botwinick recalls. "These were assets that had been misrepresented and overvalued," he says. "The banks, of course, were on the company's back."

Botwinick tried to help sell Timeplex, but he says that the then president blocked every effort. In the spring of 1977, the board brought Botwinick in as chairman and chief executive, while the president stayed on as second-in-command. "We signed a series of voting trust agreements where we would split the board. He would have three representatives and I would have three. Therefore we had to agree to get anything done.

"Well, two weeks after I was there I met with the banks. The company by then owed them $1.7 million and was losing money at the rate of thirty thousand dollars a month. They said, You have sixty days to show us how we are going to get our money back, or else." At just about the same time Botwinick learned that the client who accounted for about two-thirds of Timeplex's business had decided to shop elsewhere. "The former management had not bothered to tell me that," Botwinick says. "Meanwhile, I have hocked everything I have to buy every share I can lay my hands on.

"It was a marvelous time," Botwinick says with a hollow laugh. "We had $1.5 million in equity; $1.7 million in debt. No cash. No management. A rapidly aging product line. The major new product that the company had announced three times was still in development. In short, it was a real mess.

---

*Collect your receivables and don't worry about losing sales.*

---

"This was a company that had never sent out a statement and never dunned a customer," Botwinick recalls. "They were afraid they would lose customers if they did. Probably the most important thing I did was hire a young lady, give her a telephone and a list of people who owed us money, and told her to ask them for it. When they found out, management went into a total panic. They said, 'You can't call the customers, they're going to kick us out.' But she collected five hundred thousand dollars' worth of receivables within sixty days. Most of the customers said, 'We thought no one was ever going to call.' "

Collecting the overdue bills got the banks off Timeplex's back and gave it enough money to buy out the obstreperous president. With that, Botwinick set out to rebuild the company. "Other than the new production manager I had hired that winter, there was virtually no management in the company," he says. "There were engineers in sales and marketing. They were a bunch of loyal, hard-working people without any experience. Most of them were not very growable. There were people who were dead-ended here, or had been at other companies before coming to Timeplex. They were marginal people.

"So I started going out to search for people. However, the company still had a lousy balance sheet—although we were making money and solvent—and our facility looked like a sweatshop. Plus, I had no track record. I interviewed and interviewed and interviewed. But the only people who wanted to work here had no track record, and the ones I wanted to hire didn't want to work here. So I had to compromise. I had to hire people I didn't particularly want and promote them; in some cases they were promoted over their heads."

And Timeplex has suffered as a result, Botwinick says. The numbers prove his point. While Timeplex's most recent return on equity of 16.2 percent and net margins of 10.4 percent are in line with the industry norms, the results have been anything but consistent. Over the last five years, return on equity has varied from 8 percent to 27 percent. Long-term debt has been up and down as well. Margins, too, have been inconsistent.

Timeplex's products are fine. Its problem has been finding good people.

"You go out looking for knights in shining armor and find there are none," Botwinick says. "We have made as many mistakes as anyone else in searching for people. As a result, the management turnover has been high. We have gotten something of a reputation as a revolving door. If there is a reason for it, it may be the hiring process is too imprecise. We have tried. We have brought in outside testers to do intelligence and psychological testing. When there are professional skills involved we bring in outside professionals to do studies. The senior management interviews people repeatedly. In spite of that, our hit rate has not been very good.

"This is the real limiting factor on this company," Botwinick says. While the company now finally seems on its way—fiscal 1985 sales of $100 million could reach $175 million within two years—Botwinick laments the time it took to put everything in place. "If five years ago we had been able to attract and afford bright, educated, younger people with potential, we would be way ahead of the game today."

## Delegate Before You Have To

The frustrations of Halmos and Botwinick are both un-understandable and predictable. As small companies grow, the founder can no longer do everything himself. Many founders refuse to delegate, and their companies stop growing. Their companies never become any bigger than one person can handle.

But even for companies like SafeCard and Timeplex, which recognized the problem, the transition from individual control to broad-based management is difficult and scary. "We have gotten to the point where it is no longer just Steve and me doing everything," says Halmos. "That is a huge psychological step."

*Delegate. Most entrepreneurs don't like large organizations, and there is no reason they should try to run one.*

When do you take that step? The answer, perhaps surprisingly, is immediately upon creation. Even when the company is small enough for one person to do everything, one person should not be doing it all. Why? The answers run the gamut from practicality to human nature.

What strikes us after talking to several hundred chief executives of emerging growth companies is how few are comfortable and good at creating new ideas and also managing organizations. Maybe one in ten perform well in both roles. Some don't have the temperament—not only do they not suffer fools gladly, they are not crazy about people as bright as they are. They are not the kind of people you want handling personnel decisions.

Other entrepreneurs couldn't organize a pickup softball game, let alone a company, if their lives depended on it. And indeed their company's life does depend on it.

But the argument for early delegation of power goes beyond the entrepreneur's ability to shuffle papers and manage people. It goes to the heart of what is effective management in an emerging company.

As their companies grow quickly, entrepreneurs find they spend an increasing amount of their time dealing with minor crises, like the seventeen thousand dollars the Safe-Card manager needed to keep his house. Maybe the entrepreneur can deal with these kinds of problems with dispatch; maybe he can't. But the fact is he shouldn't have to.

What entrepreneurs are good at, by definition, is figuring out ways to compete differently; finding holes in the marketplace and ways to exploit them. That's what got them into business, not the ability to cope with a large organization. Indeed, most of these people left large organizations because they didn't like them or could not function effectively within one. If they couldn't cope with a large organization when they worked for one, how are they going to build one and run it effectively? The vast majority of them won't. Recognizing that reality, they should make plans early in their company's lives to deal with it.

Administrative tasks should be delegated as soon as the company starts to grow. It doesn't have to be anything elaborate at first. A secretary can learn how to fill out insurance forms. The person who stocks the shelves can learn about controlling inventory and ordering supplies. Ideally, those people can handle increased responsibilities as the company grows. To ensure that that happens, overqualified people should be hired for each new position as the company experiences rapid growth. The temptation is to hire cheap. That's wrong, since you'll only get what you pay for. There is also a temptation to deal with pending organizational problems by saying, "We will cross that bridge when we come to it." That's wrong too. The odds are by the time you get to the bridge, it will be too late.

Emerging growth companies emerge quickly. In addition to being able to respond to a changing market, the entrepreneur must be able to deal with the organization that will be emerging within his company as it experiences rapid growth. Business plans, either formal or informal, are drawn to deal with the outside world. Plans should also be drawn to deal with the inside world as well. That way when the organizational crisis hits—and it will—you'll be prepared. You won't have to waste time.

The specifics of the traditional business plan vary from company to company. That will be true for the plans to deal with internal growth as well. But anticipation of internal personnel and administrative problems is vital if the external business plan is to have any chance of success.

# 27

## "Get Out While You Still Have Your Marbles"

The problems of planning, staffing, and delegation of authority are easiest to see when a small company tries to pick a successor to the founding entrepreneur.

At a big company such as IBM, where the founding entrepreneur has long since left the scene, the task is relatively easy. The board of directors—frequently dominated by people who don't work for the company—chooses the successor. Often it selects the company's second-in-command, someone who has been preparing to be chief executive for a number of years. He has been groomed for the top job; his ability and dedication to the organization are well known. The outgoing chief executive of a company such as IBM may stay on the board of directors and serve, perhaps, as chairman of the finance or executive committee, but frequently he severs all ties and just retires. His nest egg in company stock, while substantial to him personally, represents less than 1 percent of the total number of shares outstanding, and he would never think of voting against the management he left behind.

Little of this holds true at small companies. And so there are problems.

First, it is the entrepreneur who decides when or if he should leave. Unlike at IBM, there is no mandatory retirement age. And even if there were, there would be no one to enforce it. The board of directors was appointed by the entrepreneur. Most often they are the top executives in the company, people he has hired. Their loyalty is to him, not the organization.

The company is the entrepreneur's life. He built it, and he is not going to let go easily, even if he knows deep down that he should. Oh, he might step down, but as he cleans out his desk he makes it clear that he plans to offer advice—some would call it meddling—from time to time. And he has made sure that advice will be heeded. He remains a controlling shareholder. So even if the founder vows he *really* is going to leave and spend the rest of his days playing with his grandchildren, he can easily step back in. And frequently—either consciously or not—he has arranged things so that he will have to come back.

---

*When you are going to step down as CEO, really step down. Go fishing. Visit the kids. But don't try to influence the company you were supposed to have left behind.*

---

Strong leaders often pick weak successors. Either they don't want the competition when they are heading the company, or—subconsciously at least—they want their legacy to last forever. What better way to ensure that your contribution will be appreciated than to have the person who follows you fail? "Old Fred sure was invaluable; nobody could fill his shoes," everyone in the organization will say.

Great for Old Fred's ego. Lousy for the company.

Other succession problems are just variations on this theme. A hard-charging executive is brought in from another, often larger, company to be second-in-command. The message is Hard Charger has been hired to create a smooth succession when Fred steps down. But Hard Charger either can't adjust to the faster-paced environment at the smaller company, as Pete Halmos talked about at Safe-Card, or he is never given any real authority as second-in-command.

And sometimes there is no transition period at all. The founder hires a new chief executive, says he is retiring, and leaves. But as he spends time with the grandchildren, puttering about the house and serving on various committees, he finds the small things that bothered him about his replacement initially have now grown into substantial problems, and he is worried about where the company is heading. He grows more frustrated daily. The result is as predictable as the sunrise.

"The Fred Corp. announced today that Hard Charger, recently named chief executive, is leaving at the end of the month, to pursue other interests," reads a press release that can be found in the *Wall Street Journal* regularly. "Former Chairman Fred will return as chief executive 'for the time being.' " Then Old Fred never leaves. Wedded to the past, he is reluctant to change anything, and more often than not, his company falls behind. Unfortunately, this is one common denominator you can find in small companies that fail to live up to their initial promise.

## A Succession Well Handled

Introspection, recognizing their own mortality, and passing the baton to new leadership are not things most entrepreneurs are good at. One exception can be found at Hunt Manufacturing, a Philadelphia-based maker of art and office supplies and specialty furniture, which has handled the transition between chief executives as well as any small company we have seen. But even at this company of $100 million sales, passing the baton posed problems, many of which still need to be resolved.

At first blush it is surprising that George Bartol III decided to step down. At sixty-one, he was as healthy as his company, which consistently turned in returns on equity of 20 percent on modest debt. Earnings and the company's stock price were rising steadily, and prospects for his Boston pencil sharpeners, Speedball arts-and-crafts supplies, and the like were strong.

And the credit for that success belonged to Bartol. The third generation to run the company, Bartol took what was once the sleepy C. Howard Hunt Pen Co. and transformed it into a company that plans to be listed in the *Fortune* 500 by 1990.

---

*If you are not certain what direction your company should take, you have little to lose by asking someone else's opinion. If you think the advice offered is dumb, you don't have to take it.*

---

The story begins in 1899 when C. Howard Hunt, who had worked for the Esterbrook Pen Co., started a firm to make pens and penpoints. He quickly went broke. Enter Georgie Bartol, Bartol's grandfather, and the forerunner of today's venture capitalists. Georgie bought troubled businesses, rebuilt them, and then sold them at substantial profits. Georgie Bartol bought C. Howard Hunt in the early 1900s with plans of turning it around and selling out. Then Georgie Bartol died.

Georgie's son, Bartol junior, received the company as part of his inheritance. The second Bartol bought the Boston pencil sharpener, a key acquisition. The sharpener, which still has a 50 percent market share, represented the first step away from pens. George the third, a history major at Princeton ("I didn't know the first thing about business"), joined Hunt upon discharge from the navy in 1946. "Hunt was then a conservative company, without any growth particularly," he recalls. "As I remember, in 1947 sales were $1.8 million or $1.9 million."

Bartol got the company moving when he began making decisions at Hunt in the early 1960s. "I decided we should take a look at our options," he recalls. "It was a family company. We didn't know what we could do with it, or what we should do with it. So we hired Arthur D. Little, at for us a very high fee, to come down and take a look at what we had. They said we had a nice, profitable business that would remain profitable. There would be lots of time to play golf. Salaries would be fine, but the company wouldn't do much.

"The option that we had, however, was to take our basic products—which were the Boston pencil sharpener and the Hunt pens—and use them as the base to convert into a growth situation," Bartol adds. "Well, it just seemed to me that if I were going to stay in the business, it wouldn't be any fun just letting it roll along. It would be more fun to see what we could do with it. That report became our long-range plan."

And, as the numbers show, Bartol implemented it successfully. So why, at age sixty-one, did he decide to step down? "It seemed to me if I hung on forever, inevitably Hunt would lose its stimulus," he says. "There may be exceptions, but nine out of ten entrepreneurial executives lose their motivation because they've made enough money or their health fails. I didn't want that to happen at Hunt."

Bartol, who, along with his family owns about 40 percent of the company's stock, also wanted to make sure that his financial investment in Hunt didn't decline. "I would rather evaluate this investment while I still have all my marbles than evaluate it when I didn't," he says candidly. "I would rather do the evaluation myself, rather than have my family or executors, who don't have the background, do it. The best way of ensuring that happens is to get out while you still have your marbles."

There was no pivotal moment that caused Bartol to step aside. Rather, it was a growing revulsion of seeing his business peers stay at the helm too long and watching their companies suffer as a result. Bartol swore that would never happen at Hunt.

But why turn the reins over to someone else? Why not simply sell out? Since neither Bartol's four daughters nor their husbands were interested in taking over the company, why not take the highest bid and play a lot of golf? At the time, Bartol could have received more than $30 million for his stock. "It is always a thought that goes through your mind, but not one I spent much time on," Bartol says. "We did cover our tracks to some degree when in July 1983, we had a secondary offering. The purpose, quite frankly, was to get a few of our eggs out of the Hunt basket so that we— the kids especially—will have a nest egg to fall back on should Hunt not prosper. Having done that, we are at the stage where we are willing and ready to take some risks."

The person who will take those risks is Ronald J. Naples, Hunt's new chief executive.

"I was looking for somebody, first and foremost, who was not interested in warm milk," Bartol says of his decision to hire Naples. "One of the reasons Ron came to a little company like Hunt instead of staying in Washington, where he could have gone to any number of major positions, was that he wanted something with excitement. I wanted somebody who felt like that and had a desire to excel. Someone with brains, and basic leadership qualities. That is a difficult thing to define, but when you see it, you know it."

He saw it in Naples. Still, Naples was not the classic choice for running Hunt.

A graduate of West Point, Naples served in Vietnam. After the army, he earned a master's in international relations from Tufts and an M.B.A. from the Harvard Business

School before he went to work in the Gerald Ford administration as a White House Fellow. The fellowship lasted a
year, and during that time Naples began to ask himself the
inevitable question, "What do you want to do for the rest of
your life?"

"I considered investment banking, which I really enjoyed
when I worked at it during the summer between semesters
at the business school. I really liked the deal-making aspects
of it, but my conclusion was I didn't want to do that for the
rest of my life. There were a couple of offers to become assistants to the chairmen of West Coast banks, but I thought
there comes a time in every man's life that you have to stop
being the bright young man and actually do something."

That something was either working as a middle manager
at a large company or going to a small (then $30 million in
sales) company named Hunt.

"I really don't think the match between what I could
bring to Hunt and what Hunt needed was very good,"
Naples recalls. Hunt had hired a headhunter whom Naples
knew casually. "We maintained an acquaintance, and
when he got the Hunt search he came to me, because he
knew I was getting ready to leave the White House. We
both concluded it probably wasn't right. Hunt was not a
high-powered organization. I had always been in pretty
large organizations; I mean, here I was leaving the White
House. And Hunt was looking for an experienced international salesman to start an international operation. I didn't
have that experience. I had an interest in international affairs, some leadership experience in the army, but no real
business experience.

"What I think happened was the recruiter was having
trouble filling the search, and he came back to me and said,
'Hey, why don't you go interview with them; you might
find it interesting,' " Naples recalls. "So I went to see them,
and the more I learned, the more interesting it became. I

could come in and be responsible for an identifiable chunk of a company and take my shot at doing something with it. When I came, it was unclear to me if this was a long-term thing or a short term, because I was very uncertain about a small organization."

Naples spent three years running the international operation and another three looking for acquisitions. The biggest one was X-Acto, a hobby knife company Hunt bought from CBS. Although Hunt had a company president, Naples reported directly to Bartol, in both jobs. It quickly became clear within Hunt that either Naples or the company president would be the next chief executive.

"I did not lose a lot of sleep over it," Naples says. "If it wasn't me, I would have some thinking to do. One day, out of the blue, George walked in and said, I have decided to make you chief executive if you want the job. The only condition was he asked me to make a ten-year commitment. I didn't think that was unreasonable. We didn't sign a contract. It was understood."

But what made Naples think he would last ten years? After all, the corporate battlefields are strewn with bright young men who were forced out of the top job. Given the circumstances at Hunt—a relatively young owner stepping down but still controlling the stock—there was an excellent chance that someday soon Hunt would be issuing a press release saying Naples "has left for personal reasons, and Bartol is resuming control of day-to-day operations." In retrospect, Naples concedes he might have been naive.

"If I had been more sophisticated, maybe I would have insisted on some kind of severance arrangement," Naples says with candor. "It was not a classic transition where the chairman leaves and says, 'Now it's your company.' I have to contend with the fact that George is still chairman, and still a major stockholder. He clearly has thoughts about this company and expectations. What makes it worse is that there is a mechanism for him to get involved if he wants. He is still chairman and active in the company—although not active day-to-day. But at the time he offered me the job, I was looking more forward to the opportunity than I was worried about the downside."

Still, it is a potential problem, and Naples knows it. "I try to do what I think is the right thing for the corporation, but at the same time I try to deal with the kinds of expectations that the board and George might have," Naples says. "Every chief executive faces this in his dealings with his board of directors. What makes it different at Hunt is that the board is not just an outside board of advisors. There are people on the board—particularly George—who have been intimately involved in the company, and he still has power in the company."

To ease that tension, Naples and Bartol talk frequently. Their most important discussion occurred right after Naples took the job, when they discovered they had a common view of Hunt's future. But they also found out they had different thoughts about how that future should be achieved. The differences boil down to this: What do you have to give up short-term to ensure long-term success?

"Everyone wants the company to do well in the long run. It doesn't do anyone any good for the company to do great this year and fall apart next," Naples says. "But the long run means different things to different people. And what is doing well enough in the short run to justify long-term success? That is probably the largest single problem that you would have in a transition like this."

Naples gives a hypothetical example. "If it's possible for Hunt's earnings to grow at 25 percent a year, by trying to do everything possible, is it correct to grow that quickly if it requires setting back projects you ought to be spending money on? Again, what is good enough? I say if we can grow 18 percent and do what we need to do, that is probably good enough year-to-year growth. The perspective on the other side may be, 'Why not do as well as we can short-term?'

"There is a classic tension between those goals," Naples says. "That tension has not been objectively resolved between us. We have to work on it. While that tension can be constructive, it does compound the complexity of my job. To be honest with you, if George wasn't there, my job would be a lot easier than it is."

There are other tensions too. "If we really are in a growth mode, there is potential for conflict in the dividend policy," Naples adds. "Clearly, the expectations of a major stockholder are one thing, and what the company needs is another." Naples says that conflict has yet to surface.

When asked if the transition has worked, Naples answers with a laugh, "I still have a job. That is probably the most basic way of answering that question. Not only do I still have a job, but I don't fear for my job over the next year. Although I am as mindful as anyone that any chief executive serves at the pleasure of the board.

"Why has it worked? I think there are three reasons. First, George and I have a common vision of what we would like the company to become. Five years from now I would be disappointed if we were not $300 million to $500 million in sales. I think we will get to $250 million to $300 million in businesses closely related to where we are. To get to $500 million, we will probably have to diversify. Is that something that we sat down and discussed? No. I think it is an understanding that grew during the six years that I worked for him.

"Another reason the transition has worked is that George had a chance to observe me over time, before he offered me the job, and I guess what he saw gave him confidence in my judgment," Naples adds. "The last reason that it has worked—to be honest with you—is that we have been successful [since Naples took over]. I don't think you can ever underestimate the importance of that."

## Don't Go Outside

From his perch, Naples is in a good position to view similar transitions that fail. Not surprisingly, he has given the matter some thought. "I think there is a problem when the chairman, who is so deeply involved in the company, all of a sudden tries to yank himself away. He finds it very difficult," Naples says. "In some sense, the fact that George has stayed on as chairman is a difficulty. It is difficult to operate truly independently with him here. But in another sense, there is a virtue to it, in that he finds a way of winding down.

"Also, I don't think it is a good idea to hire the successor from the outside," he adds. "If you have the chief executive officer picking his successor, and the CEO has enough influence to force that person to leave, then the CEO ought to have someone who not only interviews well but whose judgment, style, and philosophy he has had a chance to observe." Otherwise, says Naples, a chairman can quickly lose faith in his successor. A forced resignation is likely to follow.

---

*If you are the chief executive, but not the controlling shareholder, accept the fact there are constraints on your power—no matter what you have been promised. If you don't understand that, you are likely to be fired.*

---

It is clear that Bartol has not lost faith. He has made good on his promise of letting Naples run the company day-to-day. And Naples, who would feel more comfortable if Bartol were not there, recognizes Bartol's continuing and legitimate interest. Despite all of Naples's well-founded concerns, the transition has worked well.

Do Naples and Bartol have any advice?

"If you can get the IBM situation—where the guy serves as chairman for ten years and then truly steps down—that is probably better," Naples says with a laugh. "It is easier to do this job when you have just yourself and the board to answer to than when you have to keep someone else's expectations in mind.

"Also you have to accept intellectually that there are some constraints. Where the IBM executive can say, 'We need to broaden our equity base; we are going to issue one million new shares next year,' you can't do it without consultation. You have to accept that. If you don't, it is not going to work.

"You have to ensure there is an open and continuing frank relationship with your predecessor. George and I have made a practice of meeting regularly in an informal situation and kicking things around in general. No budgets. No agendas. No income statements. The idea is to see how things are going. 'What kinds of concerns do you have, George?' 'What kind of problems do you have, Ron? How can I be helpful, if you want me to be?' I try not to pull punches when I talk with George. I don't sugarcoat things, and I don't just talk about good things.

"The reality is if you are going to live in the cage with the gorilla, you have to make sure the gorilla is happy," Naples adds. "But the way to make sure that the gorilla is happy is not just by stroking him with the good stuff and hiding all the bad. You need to demonstrate that you are in charge, but that you understand the legitimacy of his continuing interest. If you run around saying after every time you have talked with him, 'I am running this place; he has no business looking into this stuff,' you are going to be in trouble.

"So maybe what I am saying is that it requires some self-effacing attitude," Naples adds. "You have to be true to yourself, or you won't sleep at night. But if you don't have some other considerations, you won't eat in the morning. You have to pay attention to reality."

What has made the transition immensely easier is the

fact that Bartol is not consistently hovering in the background. He has a home in Arizona, where he spends more than half the year, and he is proud of Philadelphia, where his family has been for generations, and is active in civic affairs. He is chairman of the board of the respected Franklin Museum of Science and is a director of the local Federal Reserve Board. With all that, Bartol says he has not found it hard to stay away. "I don't have the time."

Bartol feels the succession is "right on course." Instead of being a threat, he views the large block of Hunt stock his family owns as a "security blanket for Ron," meaning Naples won't have to fear a hostile takeover offer should Hunt have a down quarter or two. It makes it easier for Naples to make long-term decisions, Bartol says.

As for suggestions to other entrepreneurs, Bartol says: "I don't have any advice other than get out when you still have your marbles, and stay out."

# 28

## How to Manage Your Company's Growth

Once off and running, almost every successful entrepreneur runs into serious, unexpected problems. Even the best business plan won't anticipate everything because the marketplace keeps changing. Entrepreneurs who vault the make-or-break hurdles in this third phase of a small company's life are those who effectively use their fledgling staffs and limited resources.

The best way to do that is by recognizing from the very beginning that neither you nor your company should try to do everything itself. Those who try to go it alone—either in management or manufacturing—rarely succeed for long. By subcontracting wherever possible, you not only free up capital, but you don't waste valuable time learning another business. That is time that can be used figuring out how to compete differently. Don't worry that farming work out will cost more. By playing one contractor off another, you are guaranteed to receive a price almost as low as if you did it yourself.

And just as you delegate various components of your business to subcontractors, be prepared to delegate authority to your staff as well. Sure, it was your insight and ability that got the company started. But if you refuse to let

183

others help once the company is up and running, your company is never going to become bigger than what you can handle alone. You must build a staff.

Unfortunately, you are going to make mistakes in hiring people. It comes with the territory. However, you can reduce those problems by initially hiring people more qualified than you need. At first, they may not have enough to do. But as the company grows, they will be able to take on more responsibility. This way you'll have on hand the people you need as your company takes off. You won't have to waste time searching for them.

There are two things to remember with this strategy. First, you are going to have to pay to get the kind of people you need. You really do get what you pay for. Second, the people you hire initially may not be the best ones to be running your company five or ten years from now. Your company will change, and so will your management needs. While it is a painful realization, be prepared to bring in new—and even higher-priced—help. And at some point, earlier in the process than you will care to admit, you will have to start planning for an orderly management succession. If you plan on dying with your boots on, your company might too.

All this talk about planning for the future doesn't mean you should forget your past. A successful company remembers its early days and continues to do things as inexpensively as possible, no matter how well the company is doing. An entrepreneur shouldn't be carried away from his own success. Overconfidence is deadly. You should always run scared.

# Part IV
# ENCORE

# 29
## Once May Be Enough

"Encore! Encore!"

Those are the words every performer longs to hear. Those are also the words every entrepreneur secretly dreads to hear, because he knows how hard it will be to come up with one.

Wall Street expects every entrepreneur to have an encore. Like all true believers, it dares not countenance the thought that an entrepreneur might not have another product in the wings that's going to be at least as successful as his commercial debut.

Given one indication that the entrepreneur may not have an encore, Wall Street's dreams shatter. The stock falls like a stone. Obviously the man was not that capitalist saint, a true entrepreneur.

That is absolute rubbish. Nowhere is it written that entrepreneurs have to be eternal fountains of commercially successful new ideas. It is enough to have had one such idea and enough guts to have gone ahead and made it happen. How many other people could do even that?

More to the point, perhaps, how many others were afraid even to try? How many top executives at GM or IBM or Procter & Gamble can say they made one good commercial idea happen solely on their own initiative?

An entrepreneur's initial success can be a heady experience. Perhaps that's why most entrepreneurs who have tasted success don't quit while they're ahead. "Go for it" is their watchword. They have been richly rewarded. They're on a roll. They can do it again. Any Vegas veteran or pony player knows the feeling.

This section of *Sweat Equity* is about entrepreneurs who don't want to leave the table. It's their lucky night. They don't think they can lose.

# 30

## The Brooklyn Dodger

Let's start with a winner: Brooklyn-born Lee Rizzuto of Conair, the hair-dryer people. Rizzuto has been through it all. And he's come out ahead every time.

He's not just a survivor. Rizzuto has what you might call good bounce: The harder you throw him down, the higher he goes on the rebound. He's a streetfighter.

Rizzuto started learning the hair-care business when he started learning the alphabet. Rizzuto's mother and father had a beauty parlor at Forty-second Street and Lexington Avenue in New York City. His father had achieved a certain status in the business back in the thirties by introducing a chemical hair-curling process everyone seemed to like. Twenty years later he invented a winning hair curler, basically a spring wrapped with wire mesh that dried hair faster than existing hair curlers and conformed to the contours of the scalp so the hairdresser could achieve a better curl.

Rizzuto senior had considerable cachet in the business. People knew he was always coming up with interesting innovations. "Goodwill" the accountants would call it. But that was about all he had.

His son had bigger dreams. So after high school Leandro Rizzuto landed a job as a nighttime computer programmer for Combustion Engineering. During the day he went to New York University. He slept as you sleep in the army—any time you can.

189

It was at this point that his father came up with the better hair curler. The family was convinced they had a real winner this time. With an innovative hair curler at the core of the business they could build up a full line of accessories. But to make it happen the entire family would have to put everything it had into the new business, which they named Continental Hair Products.

So Lee quit his job with Combustion, dropped out of college, and sold his pride and joy: a new car. At the age of nineteen he took over Continental Hair—with a little coaching from his father.

Bingo! A little youthful energy mixed with a lot of contacts and an innovative product produced quick results. Soon Continental Hair was selling 10 million curlers and Japanese-made hair clips a month.

But then, just as things were looking up, disaster struck. A fire burned their warehouse to the ground. The insurance didn't even begin to cover their inventory. Rizzuto's father never really recovered from that. Two years later he died.

Pushed to the wall, Lee Rizzuto drew on every resource he had. There were quite a lot of them, actually. But sometimes a person doesn't realize this until he has to.

One thing he did know was that European trade shows could be a gold mine of new product ideas. So after his father died in 1969, a hungry Rizzuto flew across the Atlantic, looking for new ideas. Not surprisingly, perhaps, he found what he was looking for: a German-made hand-held hair-dryer. Rizzuto didn't think it worked particularly well. But he could see how to improve it right away. The important thing was there was nothing like that hand-held hair-dryer on the U.S. market. He knew his beauty-parlor customers would love it.

Upon returning home, he persuaded Japan's Mitsui to manufacture hand-held dryers of his own design—no U.S. producer could match Mitsui's prices. He knew that from long experience with hair curlers. Improving on the design of the German hair-dryers, he increased the air velocity significantly without raising the heat to the point where it would burn the hair. As a result, Rizzuto's hand-held dryers took far less time to dry hair.

One trip to Macy's did the rest. The personal-care products buyer there knew the beauty parlor supply trade as well as the consumer market. If Rizzuto's dryer was something original for beauty parlors, why not give it a newspaper ad and see what kind of response it got?

The response was over the wall. Rizzuto had a winner.

But Continental Hair was too small to capitalize on it, Rizzuto figured. The market for initial public offerings had just collapsed along with the rest of the stock market. So he trotted the idea around to the Goliaths, Gillette and Clairol, hoping to license his invention. They turned him down flat. After all, both of them had competing products that they were not about to shoot down. (Chester Carlson got the same response when he tried to interest 3M and Eastman Kodak in xerography.)

---

*Just because you can't get a major manufacturer to produce your idea under license doesn't mean it's a bad idea. The manufacturer may even be afraid of the competition it might represent.*

---

So Rizzuto decided to roll the dice, raising working capital wherever he could—from friends, customers, and suppliers. It was enough to tide him over until Continental Hair's initial public offering in 1972, when he renamed the company Conair. That done, he hedged his bets with a shrewd acquisition in the related shampoo-and-conditioner field. He bought Jherri Redding, a well-regarded wholesale name in the beauty-parlor business.

Rizzuto was on a roll. From 1970 to 1977 Conair went from $2 million in sales to $53 million and from $112,000 to $3.5 million in earnings. That was in spite of building a new plant in Edison, New Jersey, when his Japanese suppliers couldn't keep pace with demand, and a costly strike in 1977.

Then came 1978, and Conair went sailing right off the roller coaster. Conair had launched a lemon called the Pro Baby, a compact hair-dryer that stood up straight in the medicine cabinet like a bottle. Because of the strike, he didn't do any test marketing. Earnings went from a projected $5 million to a loss of $2.5 million. The $70 million sales volume Rizzuto had expected turned out to be only $40 million.

It was Rizzuto's first brush with defeat. So he spent another $2 million on advertising. But nothing happened. Pro Baby just wasn't moving off the shelves.

Now what was Rizzuto going to do with all that inventory? The last thing he needed was a write-off that would have given him another year in the red—especially when he was spending heavily to develop other new products and to install a computerized control system that took over a year and a half to debug. That one false step—launching Pro Baby without test marketing it first—was threatening to bury the company as surely as that warehouse fire had in the early days.

Rizzuto huddled with his top people and redesigned the product into a portable pistol-grip dryer that could use the Pro Baby parts. A marketing solution to a marketing mistake. It was an instant hit.

Today, under senior vice-president Salvatore DiMaschio, a veteran of Revlon, commonality of parts is the rule in every Conair dryer. Another seemingly obvious lesson was the importance of financial controls. Conair didn't really have any up until Rizzuto joined the company in 1980.

Why? Because, if demand is twice as great as supply, or "right out the door," as Rizzuto would put it, who needs inventory controls, purchasing controls, or financial planning?

By 1981 it looked as though Rizzuto and DiMaschio had bounced back. Earnings at slightly over $3 million were back up to 1977 levels—but with less leverage this time: Debt had been trimmed back and shareholder equity was a third higher than in 1977. What made the difference? Rizzuto pulled the ace up his sleeve and took the Jherri Redding line retail. It was not a new idea: other beauty parlor suppliers like Vidal Sassoon and Jhirmack had gone retail with their own beauty-salon brands before with great success. But almost nothing Rizzuto had done was original. He just improved existing ideas.

"We decided that we were not in the hair-dryer business; we were in the health and beauty aid business," says DiMaschio, repeating one of Peter Drucker's most well known suggestions: Define what business you are really in. "And what we found was that our number one position in hair-dryers gave us the leverage to market a full line very easily because the retailer would rather do business with one vendor than four vendors. And if we could supply him with comparable products across the board, this was a plus for him." That's another "obvious" point, but one Conair executed well.

How many entrepreneurs have neglected to ask themselves obvious questions because they read "obvious" to mean "trite"? One of the hallmarks of a truly successful entrepreneur, the one who is able to come up with an encore, is a certain kind of humility. He knows he needs to ask himself the obvious questions or listen to someone else ask them because he knows how often he has made mistakes.

But taking the Redding line retail was not enough at this stage to offset growing competition in Conair's core business. The company was being me-tooed by the mighty: General Electric, Gillette, and Clairol—each of which had far greater clout with the retailers. The hair-dryer market was now crowded. It was becoming doubtful whether there were any more end runs to play—and even if there were, how long would the advantage last before the corporate copiers muscled down the margins with knockoffs?

Rizzuto had tried hard to develop that elusive encore in-house at Conair, trotting out pasta machines, espresso coffee makers, and the like with little success.

Wall Street wrote him off. For years the trading record of Conair stock had looked like the electrocardiogram of a dying man—fluctuating between $1 and $2 a share. But Rizzuto kept playing for time while the Redding shampoo and conditioner line gained market share. In 1983 he added consumer telephones, updates to the Conair line, and acquired Zotos International, a top manufacturer of permanent-wave hair-care products.

---

*If you can't leverage your name recognition with an in-house product, try licensing somebody else's.*

---

Financing that acquisition may have pushed Conair's long-term debt from 10 percent of capitalization to a high 53 percent, but with Zotos's acquired earnings, Rizzuto was able to show a handsome gain in net income from $7.2 million to $13 million in 1983. Paying down that additional $46 million in debt won't be anywhere near as difficult now that Conair is making over four times as much as it was in 1981.

It will be even less difficult now that Rizzuto has bought in all of Conair's publicly traded shares. Privately held companies have no stock market incentive to show big earnings gains. Indeed, they have considerable incentive from the Internal Revenue Service to show as little earnings as possible. So a privately held Conair can afford to pay that debt down very aggressively.

No surprise, then, that at yearend 1984 Lee Rizzuto, who already owned 40 percent of Conair common, tendered for the remaining outstanding stock.

"We like the idea of competing with multibillion-dollar companies because their basic businesses are something other than personal and health care appliances," says Di-Maschio. "GE is buying RCA, and Gillette's principal business is razors, and Clairol's principal businesses are hair coloring and toiletries, and Norelco's principal business is electric shavers. So in all of these companies the personal and health care appliances divisions are sort of a stepchild. It's our principal business. Also, our business is very much a fashion business, and so the ability to move fast is quite important. We can move very quickly. We like to think we can be the second company out in any new successful product in our category. We may not invent it, because we're not engineering types. We're sales and marketing types. But once that product is established as successful, we can be the second company on the shelf because we can move faster than the competition. So we take none of the risks of inventing but still can get the rewards of any new product that is introduced."

Example: L'Oréal pioneered a styling hair-care product called Mousse, which looked like the dessert in question when sprayed from its aerosol can. It was the hottest product in beauty salons in 1982. When L'Oréal took the product retail in 1983, Mousse went from $0 to about $150 million in sales in one year. In January of 1984, Conair was on the shelf with its Mousse. It wasn't until several months later that Revlon and the others got on the shelf with their versions. But by then it was too late. "Once you tie up that real estate in the store, the retailer doesn't have room for that next guy that's coming along," says DiMaschio. "In order to put you on he's got to take someone else off. So we'll spend a disproportionate amount of our promotional dollars to be first, second, or third. We don't organize our company for lowest cost of production. We try to structure ourselves so we can market the product fastest."

With five distinct but closely related product groups as a base, and a much-strengthened retail reputation, and a survival instinct worthy of scrutiny by Charles Darwin, one can hardly blame Lee Rizzuto for reaching for the brass ring.

Now let's examine a few of the pitfalls that a successful emerging growth company can expect to face when trying to stay in the game not just for nine innings, but for this and coming seasons. The first question has to be "Why bother?" Why not sell out after you hit it big with your original idea?

The answer may have a lot to do with how old you are when you ask it. Things have a way of looking quite a bit different when you're in your early sixties, than when you're fifteen or twenty years younger—like Lee Rizzuto. And, as we said at the outset, when you've done it once there's a natural tendency to think you can do it again.

But asking yourself "Why bother?" is always an intelligent starting point, especially if by trying for that encore you might be endangering the hard-won family nest egg.

After all, who can better appreciate the risk of entrepreneurial endeavors than someone who has done it himself? There are times, if he is sincerely thinking of the welfare of his family, when he must admit that cashing in his chips is perhaps the most responsible thing he can do. And, of course, that man's reluctant retreat can be another's brave new world of opportunity.

# 31

## The Classic LBO

As initially conceived, a suitable candidate for a leveraged buyout was thought to be a small, slow-growing company with a well-maintained plant and a secure niche in its market. The venture capitalist and the lending banker wanted a highly predictable order stream to borrow against. A slow-growing company was preferable because they didn't want its cash flow diverted for the capital spending needed to meet soaring demand. The bankers wanted the entrepreneur to cut back sharply on capital spending for a while so he could use that cash flow to pay off the debt as rapidly as possible. Since his company dominated its market, he wouldn't have to worry unduly about the competition while he was paying off the bank.

Such companies are not all that common, of course. And neither were LBOs ten years ago. They were essentially a way for a capable executive with little capital to buy a family company, a company perhaps that no one else wanted, after the founder died.

But suppose the cash-strapped buyer didn't have to worry about the prudent concerns of that venture capitalist and the banker. Suppose he could just issue high-interest (and high-risk) "junk bonds" to finance the buyout and sell those risky securities easily to an eager public, which had fallen in love with their high rates in a sudden deflationary environment. That would mean that almost anyone could buy almost any company with very little cash down by borrowing against its future cash flow. They could even offer to sell off some of its existing divisions as a "down payment." The public, consciously or unconsciously, was saying it was willing to take the risk.

So tempting was that idea that the concept has since been grossly abused. Today the technique is used on companies with far less certain future cash flows and of far greater size. The resultant accretion of debt on corporate balance sheets has become quite worrying.

At a time when so many small companies are being acquired in leveraged buyouts by would-be entrepreneurs, often as a result of "restructuring" programs in major corporations, we offer a cautionary tale: a look at a perfectly conceived and executed LBO that has managed to survive the kind of trying times that are merely typical of any LBO—a fact they won't be quick to tell you on Wall Street.

Do you think today's LBOs would be able to weather these kinds of risks, let alone flourish as Ted Schad's has done?

Glamorous, Lou-Ana Foods wasn't. Back in 1971 it was a marginal little vegetable oil mill down in the Cajun country of Opelousas, Louisiana, doing about $26 million of business a year. The factory walls were infested with termites. The equipment, although well maintained, was aging and cantankerous—some machines literally had to be kicked every now and then, or they would stall. A forest of weeds had overgrown tons of rusting scrap metal in one part of the factory yard. Slow-moving workers answered "I don't know" with alarming frequency.

"It looked like hell," says the buyer, Ted Schad.

To make things worse, the owner—a cranky ninety-two-year-old named Jesse Barnet—wanted $2 million cash for the place.

But Schad was interested. The firm specialized in low-volume vegetable oils (i.e., peanut oil, cottonseed oil, and palm oil). It was a niche of sorts, Schad realized—mainly because Lou-Ana's oils could often be substituted at less cost for soybean oil, which accounts for 65 percent of the U.S. vegetable oil market. There were no heating bills to eat into profits in the winter. Plus there was no research spending to worry about. This wasn't a high-tech company where overnight product revolutions could make a toboggan slide out of its pricing structure. Lou-Ana's control system was virtually nonexistent, meaning there would be plenty of cost-cutting opportunities. Its location was ideal—halfway between the port cities of Houston and New Orleans, near an interstate highway, and with no fewer than three railways crossing the plant's property. Plus the work force was stable and relatively inexpensive, by national standards.

---

*The original, modest concept of what constituted an ideal leveraged buyout is still possible and still a good idea.*

---

A veteran of Sunkist and Van Camp Seafood (Chicken of the Sea tuna), and later a food industry consultant at the accounting firm of Peat Marwick Mitchell, Schad knew the business well. He also knew what he wanted in an LBO. Lord knows he'd tried often enough to do one.

But Schad was on a consulting assignment for McIlhenny & Co., the Tabasco sauce people. There, in the antebellum splendor of Avery Island off the Louisiana coast, Schad was trying to interest ex-Marine General McIlhenny in diversifying. He spoke eagerly of the opportunities at Lou-Ana, with its high-quality but abysmally marketed product —an opportunity for a well-known national brand like Tabasco sauce. Cost-cutting opportunities could fill a book.

General McIlhenny listened attentively and then spoke his piece: Here was Schad trotting around the country telling every chief executive who would listen what to do. Schad was always saying what he really wanted to do was run his own company. He had toyed with buying sixty-two of them, only to back away each time. Well, here was his chance to buy the company of his dreams. Why didn't Schad stop sitting on the sidelines? Why didn't he buy this company? Or wasn't he really serious about wanting his own company?

It was just the kind of "put up or shut up" challenge Ted Schad says he needed to make him take the plunge. But all he could scrape together at the time was thirty thousand dollars—a far cry from $2 million.

In many ways Schad was in the same position that an executive vice-president of Lou-Ana might have been in. He knew the business well and had good ideas about how to grow the company, but he had no capital. He was just the kind of buyer for whom LBOs were initially designed.

Once McIlhenny convinced him to go ahead with the Lou-Ana buyout, Schad discovered raising the money would be the least of his troubles. As a consultant he'd advised others on such deals often enough. So Schad knew what to do. First, he talked another Peat Marwick partner, now deceased, into investing with him in Lou-Ana. He then approached the maverick Wall Street investment banking firm of Oppenheimer & Co., which specialized in smaller LBO deals at the time. He convinced Oppenheimer to back him. Oppenheimer's backing in turn made it easy to tap large lenders like The Fidelity Mutual Life Insurance Co. for the bulk of the payment.

Now came the hard part—solving those problems Schad had described to McIlhenny as opportunities. Most of them were quite basic. But, of course, that didn't mean that all Schad had to do was snap his fingers and away they would go.

For example, Lou-Ana's books were kept on a cash basis.

While Schad rushed to recruit the people who could set up a proper double-entry bookkeeping system so that he could get a handle on costs, he had to struggle for five long months trying to run the place on a daily inventory statement. That, he said, was like trying to fly a 747 without instruments.

Pilferage had become a sort of expected right of employment. The company gas pump was never locked, for example. So employees routinely stopped at it to fill up their cars and pickups. Laxness in other areas was abused also. Since there was no purchasing agent, when corporate supplies were short, employees would just run into town and sign the company name. Schad found twenty or thirty different signatures on company purchase slips. Not surprisingly, Lou-Ana Foods didn't always get the best price.

All told, Schad figures he saved seven hundred thousand dollars the first year just locking things up and making people sign for things they took.

As his new accounting systems began spitting out numbers, Schad tackled the harder task of closing down marginal businesses and laying off workers. That was not an easy task in a little town where there weren't many other employers. For a while he could put surplus labor to work cleaning up the factory yard. But the real solution to the surplus labor problem was to grow. And that meant getting his costs down.

So Schad spent heavily on equipment. He bought a continuous-acidulation machine, a continuous bleaching system, a quality-control lab.

He could afford to, of course. He didn't have to show ever-increasing earnings to please Wall Street. His only audience was the Internal Revenue, and its interest in Lou-Ana's taxable income was quite different. So Schad plowed everything back.

Since his competitors would be the big food industry giants, Schad also spent heavily on people who knew how the big food companies operated—and where their weak spots were. Lou-Ana's senior vice-president for finance and administration had been the assistant controller of the Post division of General Foods. Schad's production chief and his technical services man came from Procter & Gamble. His director of engineering came from Norton-Simon's Hunt-Wesson division. The manager of bulk sales came from Swift. The corporate development manager came from Rockwell International, and the commodity trader, a critical position, from Lever Brothers.

To lure these men Schad offered a stock appreciation rights plan keyed to assets. Says Schad: "Their stock does everything my stock does except two things: One, it can't vote; and two, they don't pay for it. When they hear the second part it overcomes their objections to the first part in a hurry." Since Lou-Ana's stock redemption rights are tied to book value, Lou-Ana executives share Schad's enthusiasm about plowing back profits into fixed assets.

---

*One advantage to being a privately held company is that the tax system encourages you to spend money on plant and equipment.*

---

Still, recruiting top executives to a town like Opelousas, Louisiana, provoked more than a few amused remarks about Dogpatch. "I was out in a cocktail party in L.A. when someone asked me, 'Where in the hell is Opelousas?'" Schad recalls. "Well, someone picked up on it, and now we have tee-shirts that say, 'Where in the hell is Opelousas?' You'd be amazed at some of the comments when we wear them. 'Are you a Third World country?' Or they'll say, 'I thought it was spelled Appaloosa, you know, like the horse.' It's really comical."

Schad takes such joking in stride and tries to persuade the would-be recruit and his wife to pay a visit to Opelousas. "It does wonders for his wife to be sitting next to a wife who last lived in New York and seems to be happily settled into the community."

Soon Lou-Ana's board also sported major corporate names: William Karnes, former chief executive of Beatrice Foods; Howard Phillips from Oppenheimer and formerly Norton Simon's acquisitions man; Sanford Kaplan, formerly chief administrative officer at Xerox.

But there were plenty of unanticipated problems along the way as well. In 1974 President Nixon introduced price controls, and Lou-Ana Foods took a bath. When Lou-Ana Foods came roaring back with record profitability in the commodity boom of 1975 there was no new-issues market for Oppenheimer and Fidelity to cash in their chips. So Schad had to buy out his original backers himself, again by leveraging the company's future earnings.

By mid-1979, after paying off his bankers and venture capitalists, he stopped to smell the roses: He now owned 100 percent of a company doing $60 million a year. He could show a return on equity of over 40 percent with little debt. And the appraised value of the company's assets had gone from $2 million to $13 million since 1975.

Then the Carter administration introduced a grain embargo in 1980 just after Lou-Ana had doubled its production capacity. Overnight Schad found himself operating in the red at one-third of capacity. "The world had not forgotten Nixon," says Schad. "So that grain embargo really shut down our export markets overseas. We were exporting around $13 million at the time. Later, after the embargo was lifted, there wasn't a chance to woo them back because the dollar escalated out of sight."

Recently, Lou-Ana was doing $115 million in sales. Its appraised asset value was up to $22 million. Profitability has suffered of course, with a major farming crisis aggravated by a global commodity glut. "The highest return on equity we've hit in the past three years is 16 percent," says Schad. "This year we might get as high as 19 percent. Even so, Lou-Ana's returns, while powered by slightly higher debt leverage than is typical in the food industry, still rank as a clearly superior performance.

"Of course, I'm worried about growing the equity and not showing fancy returns," says Schad with a slight smile. "We've done a great deal of capital spending during this period. We have computerized both our plant and our office. We have totally automated our packaging department, placing an automated warehouse next to it. We also converted from glass bottles to plastic bottles—all in an effort to lower our costs. You see, we're as large as you need to be to achieve all the known economies of scale. We have also plowed profits back into ever more highly specialized people and into new programs. We're coming out with a first—two nonvegetable oil–based consumer products. We've also brought in a nutritionist to set up a test kitchen, develop recipes and cookbooks, provide dietary information—that sort of thing. And then we have greatly upgraded a quality-control program."

Years of consulting experience warned him against the kind of "gold plating" overspending many private companies indulge in on the belief that if they don't spend it, Uncle Sam will just tax it away. Schad: "My overriding concern has been that we would move so fast in computerization, for example, that we would end up with a mess on our hands."

Now Schad is thinking about acquiring some other companies. "We've come close a couple of times to buying another food company outside the vegetable oil business," he says. "Our industry has suffered from overcapacity for six years. We want to be a niche marketer. It's what I was trying to persuade the late General McIlhenny to do back in 1971. I mean a major grain trader like Cargill is 380 times our size! There's no way we're ever going to be able to take them on head-to-head."

In the same circumstances many smaller companies go the private-label route, manufacturing at a steep discount for high-volume orders. Often it looks like a comparatively easy way to grow a business rapidly. But Schad thinks that's a dangerous game. "We have gone 180 degrees in the opposite direction," he says. "For example, our food service business is 96 percent branded. It's much slower to build a business this way, but my feeling is that the proprietary aspects of a brand are worth it. In the private-label business if you want it bad enough, and I've got it, you can take it away from me by just dropping your price."

---

*The private-label route can look like quite an appealing way to grow quickly. But often it only makes you more vulnerable, with no hope of achieving the profitability you need to grow.*

---

How can Lou-Ana launch a branded product in competition with the giant food companies? Schad, a proud alumnus of Virginia Military Institute, likens his strategy to an airborne assault behind enemy lines. "I don't have the resources of Procter & Gamble, so I can't launch a full-scale assault on Normandy Beach where you throw everything in the book at them. I go in like the paratroopers do. I drop behind the lines with a highly specialized oil and build up advertising gradually, often with a salesperson who knows the territory like the back of his hand. Usually our competitors aren't aware we're there. And let's say the last place you saw me was in Alabama. The next place you'll see me reappear may be Florida—anywhere there's a weakness, where no one is really tending the store. Where everyone is kind of rolling along complacently."

Ask Ted Schad the most important thing he's learned from all this, and you get a familiar answer: "The biggest difficulty an entrepreneur has is learning to delegate and let go," he replies without hesitation. "Back in 1975, three of my senior people and I attended an American Management Association seminar for senior management, and their instructor spotted that right away. He and I talked for three hours after class, and I came back a changed man. You know, it's hard to let go—I don't care how broad-minded you've been, or how many years you've been a consultant and have criticized other people for making the same mistake. It's still not your money that's at risk."

The point is an entrepreneur often fares better when he tries to unleash the entrepreneur in others. In politics or in business it usually seems easier, and more effective, to dictate than to delegate. But all of us are human. "No one man's mind is sufficient to grasp the entire truth," wrote English political scientist John Stuart Mill over a hundred years ago. That reminder of human limitations was intended as an endorsement of the parliamentary process, but it would serve as well as an endorsement of delegation. By not delegating responsibility before 1975 Ted Schad very nearly stifled the company's growth as surely as old Jesse Barnet had done. There were simply too many important decisions that needed to be made, and no one man could make them all intelligently. The trouble is delegating responsibility inevitably means letting other people make mistakes.

# 32

## "It's Like Selling Religion on a Streetcorner"

One of the many Smith families in Cleveland, Ohio, once controlled and managed a rotary-brush and foundry molding machine company called Osborn Manufacturing. From humble origins making horseshoe-cleaning brushes, the company by the dawn of the sixties had become by far the largest producer in both markets and was averaging returns on equity of close to 30 percent, with a totally clean balance sheet, on sales of nearly $20 million.

As then-president and chief executive Norman F. Smith remarked at the time, there was rather obviously an insufficient draw on Osborn's cash. That's a self-deprecating way of saying the company was a little money machine—the master of two market niches.

Osborn followed the Eastman Kodak philosophy: Make your money on the film, not the camera. Give them the camera at little more than cost so they'll buy film, which gets used up quickly. Cameras can last decades. For Osborn, the main event was selling as many rotary brushes as possible. If you have to custom-design finishing machines for every customer in order to do it, then go right ahead. Don't try to make money on that machine. Instead, ask the customer how he's getting rid of metal burrs and rough edges after machining, stamping, or welding operations. Why not brush them off to avoid damage to product components like aerospace parts, which must be manufactured to close tolerances? "We'd be happy to design a machine ourselves for you that would do that." It was a persuasive pitch.

Smith even had a large recreational vehicle made over into a mobile demonstration unit to reinforce the pitch. The latest Osborn machines were inside with sales support technicians clad in Osborn shop aprons (which they seldom wore in the Cleveland factory) inside to have a go at the prospect's semifinished components.

Then came a curse disguised as a blessing: Osborn research came up with a plastic grinding wheel. Osborn had long used rubber and plastic bonding materials in its rotary brushes to prevent the bristles or wires from flaying at the ends. Then they started adding abrasive elements for jobs that required more metal removal. One day someone said, "If you take out the bristles and add more abrasive, guess what you have?" The answer, of course, was a plastic grinding wheel.

That was almost all you had to say if you were in the business. Ordinary grinding wheels are actually a vitreous or glasslike product. Drop a tool on them accidentally, which is quite easy to do, and they can shatter while spinning. The danger, of course, is that with all that centrifugal force the shard would fly off like a bullet. A plastic grinding wheel would certainly be safer.

Then there's durability. Friction breaks the abrasive elements off ordinary grinding wheels fairly easily. The hardened vitreous matrix cracks, and off comes the abrasive with it. Now put that same abrasive into a polyurethane matrix as Osborn had done, and the abrasive lasts significantly longer because the plastic matrix allows the abrasive to revolve in place and get smaller, not fly off.

So the plastic grinding wheel, which Osborn engineers named Ramron—or Norman (for President Norman Smith) spelled backward, more or less—was safer and longer-lasting. "You could also run the wheel at higher speeds safely," says Smith. "That was one of the big things."

It seemed too good a product to ignore. It was an encore for Osborn that had bubbled up naturally from research just the way you would want it to. To Smith it also seemed too potentially big a product for Osborn to try to market with its own sales force. The major grinding wheel manufacturers, such as Norton and Carborundum, were over ten times Osborn's size. Even smaller Bay State Abrasives was a giant in comparison with Osborn. Threaten them by taking away any of their big customers, and they could price Ramron right out of the market before it had time to win any significant market share.

More to the point, perhaps, was the cost of butting up against a commodity product like grinding wheels. Even if Smith put a premium price on Ramron, trying to carve out a niche at the high end of the market, the number of salespeople that required was daunting. And what if Ramron bombed?

---

*Entrepreneurial product ideas can arise when you're not ready for them—as when you're ready to retire and sell off a very profitable company.*

---

Smith was near retirement age. He planned to sell the closely held little company to a larger, far more widely held company to spare his family difficult valuation problems with the Internal Revenue Service when estate taxes were levied. To place the serious burden of an ambitious and costly Ramron marketing effort on Osborn's splendid earnings at this point seemed counterproductive even if it were eventually a stunning success. It would surely make Osborn less salable short-term.

But Smith couldn't just walk away from Ramron either. Surely there was some way to launch the product without forcing Osborn to leave the lucrative security of its niches. Smith pinned his hopes on trying to license larger manufacturers to market it for him. First he approached the big grinding wheel manufacturers themselves. While they professed to be quite impressed by the Ramron technology after studying its performance at some length in their research labs, the licensing negotiations dragged on interminably. Finally Smith approached large machine tool manufacturers in Cleveland, but there too negotiations dragged on forever.

Why was this happening? Were the other companies just trying to wait out the Ramron patents?

"We did go into the business in a small way and tried to specialize in jobs where we'd have big volume and little sales cost," Smith says. "And we had some success. Our largest customer at the time was Caterpillar. They are known for their willingness to try out all sorts of new products. If they could save money by using Ramron, they'd do it. A lot of companies wouldn't go to that much trouble. Caterpillar had a great reputation for knowing their business when it came to manufacturing. So they tried it out and used it, and they became by far our largest customer. So we had a modest success. We were selling, I suppose, $2 million worth of Ramron wheels by the time we sold Osborn to Sherwin Williams."

That was in 1967, near the height of the great bull market of the sixties. Thereafter Osborn was tossed like a piggy bank from then-ailing Sherwin Williams to Giddings & Lewis to Canadian-owned AMCA.

And what became of Ramron, that star-crossed product?

Hollywood would entitle it *Against All Odds*. "Ramron was sold to some of the individuals in the Ramron operation. "I've always thought that if Ramron had come along when I was still in my fifties we could have made it go," says Smith. "But we were getting to the point that I was too old. I had to get out of the business. And there was nobody that had a top job down there who was inspired by my conviction. It's not an unusual thing to happen. I think many times if somebody high up in the organization doesn't get a hold of a product and get enthused about a new idea, it won't go anywhere. It takes somebody who has enough weight to push things to get the company to do it. If the only people who believe are way, way down the line, you don't get very far. A lot of people get their nose out of joint because they're jealous: jealous of the product and jealous of the people who believe in it. But you've got to be a believer to sell a new product. It's like selling religion on a streetcorner. You have to be a believer, or you aren't going to get anywhere. I can tell you there were at Osborn quite a few people who almost hoped that Ramron wouldn't work. Wasn't their idea. Not invented here. Nothing our research department liked better than to say about new product ideas generated outside their department than, 'Well they're always coming up with some screwballed idea.'

"There's an awful lot of competition in any organization, and I think that the research department has an awful lot of trouble with the operating part of the business. That's why the big guy has to get behind it and push it."

# 33

## Dead-End Niche?

Of course, many more entrepreneurs in their sixties sell outstanding baby blue-chip companies without ever having been able to find a potential encore like Ramron.

About thirty years ago, Fred Godley and Lawson Reed spotted a new product idea at a chemical engineering trade show that fired their entrepreneurial spirit: a Teflon-lined valve.

It was an ordinary plug valve—basically a shaft with a hole drilled in the middle, seated in a hollow globe divided into two hemispheres. One quarter-turn of the valve left the hole open between the two chambers, and liquid flowed. One quarter-turn more, and the valve was shut. This was hardly new. Similar valves were found in the ashes of Pompeii.

What was new was the Teflon lining. That made the valve impervious to highly corrosive chemicals, since Teflon is chemically inert to many of them. That was an important breakthrough back in 1956, when petrochemicals were looked upon as a growth industry. Better still, Teflon's constantly slippery surface (originally intended as a friction-reducing lining for naval rifles) also eliminated the need for costly lubrication.

Lawson and Reed also spotted the advantage of being able to mold Teflon into complex shapes for far less than it would cost to machine a similar shape.

The trouble was that Teflon, a new product, was not at all easy to work with. It would crack under the changes of temperature that a valve of this sort could be expected to endure. (Engineers Godley and Reed soon figured out the need to design in room for Teflon to expand and contract with temperature change.) Worse, there was a sizable investment required to make the molds.

Instead of being discouraged, Godley and Reed thought a fussy product was just perfect. In their midthirties at the time, they were experienced enough to recognize that the very difficulty of manufacturing such a valve was a marvelous protection: a niche waiting to happen, if you will. A small market plus difficult manufacturing would automatically limit the competition.

---

*A specialized product idea that discourages its inventor because it's so hard to manufacture can, if you can master it, become a niche also.*

---

And they had a card up their sleeves: Teflon was made by E. I. du Pont de Nemours—the company that invented sales support and "pull through" advertising (du Pont would pay a substantial portion of the advertising costs for final products that used its materials). People in the business knew that du Pont would hold any customer's hand as long as it needed to be held.

Godley's fondest recollection about du Pont's help was the time he told a skeptical potential customer to call du Pont directly to check out the feasibility of the new valve Godley was trying to sell him. The customer called du Pont and got Irenée du Pont himself, a top member of the founding du Pont family. He happened to be the applications engineer for Teflon. Godley made the sale.

So Godley and Reed contacted the inventor, Deas Sinkler. Sinkler, quite flattered by their interest, agreed to join the company. But Sinkler was a restless soul who enjoyed inventing more than manufacturing. A few years later he left.

Then came Practical Lesson No. 1 for the former roommates at Hotchkiss and Yale (whose wives even managed to get pregnant simultaneously). Not long after Xomox (as they named their company) got started, the president of a far larger valve company called to give them a "friendly" lecture on pricing. Roughly translated, it was "Undercut me and I'll blow you out of the water." But he put it more gently, says Godley—something like "If you have a new product, don't discount it and invite more competition than you can handle right in the beginning. Instead, set your price above your competitor's. If you think you're making too much money, it's only because you don't yet have the support systems you will soon need if the product is popular."

Ironically, that self-serving bit of "advice" from the competition was good just the same. The reason it was good advice was that Godley and Reed had a proprietary product with inherently superior characteristics that the market was willing to pay a premium for. Had Xomox been producing commodity valves like most of the other three-hundred-odd companies then in the industry, it would have been terrible advice.

Godley and Reed took the advice. As a result Xomox averaged a close to 30 percent return on equity for two decades. You could call it a triumph of imaginative product engineering: Godley and Reed replicated the original Sinkler valve into literally thousands of different variations, all custom-designed for clients.

There were temptations along the way, as there always are if you're successful. In the beginning, many far larger manufacturers would offer to sell the Xomox valves under exclusive license all over the United States. In a sense it was a trade-off question. What would you rather have: a short-term increase in volume and royalty income or, by keeping all future profits for yourself, a long-term increase in shareholder equity that would give you a real future?

Lawson and Reed certainly tried to build a company that would endure. Diversification was the vogue in the sixties, and Xomox flirted with a specialized filter developed by Monsanto to remove particles of matter as small as a micron. The idea was not unlike Lee Rizzuto's Jherri Redding ploy. Market someone else's product and use the cash flow to integrate backward into manufacturing. Trouble was, Monsanto's filter wasn't able to perform as well as Godley and Reed had been led to believe. Scratch one attempted diversification.

Du Pont brought them an idea for an artificial hip joint that needed a manufacturer with a sophisticated knowledge of how to work with Teflon. That led to a nice little business making bone substitutes for the middle ear.

There were some encores, but none equal to the original. In 1970 they came up with a new type of actuator (the device that powers valves) that was as difficult to make as Sinkler's valves and as elegant in its simplicity. Eventually—after a lot more development work than either had anticipated—it became a good product for Xomox. But not good enough to open new horizons for the company.

A bit later they came up with an artificial heart valve, but then stopped the project when they realized that it would take too much engineering and marketing time away from their main effort. As always their encores were endless permutations of the Teflon-lined valves.

By 1979 the company had a mature product line. The competition was getting rougher. And the founders were in their sixties. They thought they could diversify by acquisition. They bought the Atwood & Morrill division of Foster Wheeler, which made valves for the energy industry big enough for a man to walk through. The trouble was they bought the company just before the oil market fell apart.

So in mid-1981 Godley and Reed cashed in their chips and sold out to Emerson Electric. It is hard to see how they could have done better, either for themselves or, just as important to them, for the people who worked for Xomox.

---

*There's nothing wrong with cashing in your chips and saying, in effect, "I had only one commercial idea." You can always change your mind later.*

---

There are a couple of morals to this story. One is that a hard-to-make, fussy product with a highly specialized market may make a perfect niche, but in time it also may be a cul-de-sac that leads nowhere else. Another is that you can make a very nice living for your entire working life figuring out every last product development from such an idea. When you have exhausted your line extensions you can sell out.

Again, there's nothing wrong with cashing in your chips without ever really having found an encore. There may not be one—or at least not one that you and your organization can afford.

# 34

## The Fast Track

Dermot Dunphey of Sealed Air, a hungry Irishman with degrees from both Oxford and the Harvard Business School, was a favorite of the gods virtually from birth at least in one respect: He was well connected with some top Wall Street deal makers and venture capitalists early in his career.

It was right at the top of the sixties bull market in 1968 when Wall Street's young wunderkind of the era, Donaldson Lufkin & Jenrette, first met young Dunphey. The investment bankers at DLJ were favorably impressed with the fact that while still in his late twenties Dunphey had managed a leveraged buyout of a small packaging company, which he had been invited to turn around by the company's eighteen shareholders. Opportunities like that do not come along every day, not even to Harvard Business School graduates.

Then Dunphey had turned around and sold the little packaging company to Hammermill Paper at a tidy profit and had invested part of the proceeds with DLJ. "My timing was all wrong—it was the top of the market—so the value of my investment declined!" Dunphey recalls. "It wasn't their fault, but it was probably the most costly personnel fee anyone has ever paid!"

Personnel fee? Well, to DLJ, Dunphey looked like just the

man to bail out one of their start-ups called Sealed Air, another packaging company that had just plunged into the
red. Impatient for results in a rapidly deteriorating market,
DLJ, which owned a controlling 45 percent of Sealed Air
(venture capitalists do not come cheap), simply put Dunphey on the board as its representative.

Perhaps it should come as no surprise that shortly thereafter Sealed Air's president resigned because of persistent
criticism from the board and that the board then turned
to—you guessed it—Dermot Dunphey.

Dunphey found himself in clover. He is the first to admit
that his predecessor had put together an excellent management team. His product was proprietary and full of potential: bubbles of air encapsulated in neat little rows as an
intrabox packaging material. In large part, the red ink had
been caused not by falling sales, but by heavy investment
in a new manufacturing process—a process that Dunphey
was the first to call "very beneficial."

If his predecessor did everything right, why, then, was he
put under so much pressure that he resigned? Well, says
Dunphey, the man hadn't cut back soon enough on a lot of
expansion programs in the downturn of 1970 because he
had no contingency plan.

Whatever the reason, Dunphey in textbook fashion
rolled over the company's heavy short-term debt load with
a five-year consolidation loan and installed a financial
planning system. He also cut back research. Company momentum did the rest.

For most of the seventies, Sealed Air averaged close to a
20 percent return on equity, with low debt, and its earnings
grew 28 percent a year.

But Dunphey was concerned. The bubble wrap market
was beginning to look as if it had been just about saturated.
Sealed Air had just attempted an encore—a swimming
pool blanket that warmed the water beneath when the sun

warmed the little bubbles. But that product was hardly an Ivory soap that would generate huge cash earnings for generations to come.

Many, lacking Dunphey's sophisticated Wall Street contacts, might have thought that the end of the line. But Dunphey had DLJ's venture capital head, John Castle, on his board always reminding him—if only by his very presence—of how lucky Dunphey had been to be handed such an opportunity.

So Dermot Dunphey of Oxford and Harvard did just what Lee Rizzuto of Brooklyn did: He bought time by acquiring promising little companies in closely related fields. With his contacts at DLJ, it was perhaps a bit easier for Dunphey to make his moves—but the important thing is he made the right ones—and at the right times.

In 1976, largely on borrowed money, he bought Instapak, which had $11 million in sales. The company was half Sealed Air's size and had come up with a gun that shot insulating urethane foam, which expands dramatically on contact with air, into any container. Instapak turned out to be a superb packaging material for sophisticated electronic devices and other sensitive apparatus needing particular care in packaging.

Over the next five years, Instapak's sales, with the benefit of Sealed Air's more seasoned sales force, quadrupled while bubble wrap grew just 50 percent.

By mid-1980, Sealed Air common jumped from six to nearly sixteen. Wall Street was seduced. Dunphey wasn't a one-product entrepreneur, analysts told themselves. He was putting together a marketing-driven specialty packaging company. And just look at the record: Earnings and sales had quadrupled in five years.

Having a higher price-earnings multiple on Sealed Air stock helped Dunphey, of course. Now he had the liquidity of fairly heavily traded shares to offer smaller entrepreneurs who were still trapped in their niches. So in 1983 Dunphey bought Cellu Products, which had $43 million in sales and imaginative, proprietary insulating packaging for bottles.

Again, the company was half Sealed Air's size, so it made an immediate and significant impact on Sealed Air's results. And the product line was closely related so the sales force was only strengthened by the move.

---

*Just because you're small doesn't mean you can't grow by acquisition. You can even help finance that acquisition by selling off one of its divisions—just as the well-publicized raiders do.*

---

"We sold off one-third of it immediately," says Dunphey. "We sold a tissue paper segment that had nothing to do with our core business." That dramatically lowered the effective price of acquiring the product Dunphey needed to fill a gap in his product line. "They also had a proprietary technology for a product called Drylock, a pad that absorbs liquids in supermarket meat trays."

Why did Cellu Products want to sell to Sealed Air? "The man who owned it 100 percent was ready to cash in—happens all the time," says Dunphey. "He was fifty years old, but he had worked incredibly hard, and he recognized he was worth $20 million on paper and he wanted to realize that. I think he also had the wisdom to realize that his talents were better suited to running smaller companies. Cellu had gotten to the size where it wasn't any fun anymore. Now he's got himself another company he's hoping to make another $20 million out of. I made him a director of Sealed Air. He's a pretty good guy."

In 1984 Dunphey followed up by acquiring a company of $1.5 million sales—Cortec, which made another type of insulating material that protected against vapor corrosion.

Then he worked out a deal to market other insulating materials made by far larger Bemis Co., which shield against electrostatic discharge.

"These two steps were designed to expand our business mission from providing protection to our customers from damage caused by shock, vibration, and abrasion, which is what our packaging business always did, including protection from two other elements of hostile environment: corrosion and electrostatic discharge," Dunphey explains. "Such discharges are a problem that has grown dramatically in the last few years with the miniaturization of electronic components. Basically our business now has a protection concept."

When you consider how badly high-technology stocks have been battered, it is indeed a tribute to Dunphey that Sealed Air stock has marched steadily upward. Recently, its price-earnings multiple was at a 50 percent premium over the market as a whole. As was the case with Textron 20 years earlier, Wall Street could see the wisdom of collecting niche-master companies in closely related businesses that have high margins.

And what does Dunphey feel he's learned from all this? The words come slowly and seem to surprise him: "The two most important elements are first to develop the capacity for strategic thinking about your business—that's quite different from strategic planning. What I'm talking about is having a vision of the business that you are continually updating. That means you can't fall in love with any products or any market. There are a lot of companies that fall in love with their own particular innovation or technology or market, and life passes them by. People identify themselves more and more with their big success in life. But the truth is you earn your spurs every day. The marketplace doesn't care that you made a great breakthrough five years ago. It's what can you do for me now?

"The second thing is people," Dunphey goes on. "You have to have a sort of Marine Corps philosophy of being the best. You have to make it possible for your people to combine financial rewards with the psychic rewards of being associated with a winner."

The hard part, of course, is not falling in love with your first winning product. If you want to try to repeat your first success, then you can't look back. You must be willing to go through all the anxiety and effort that starting again always entails.

# 35
## Tiger by the Tail

Fate sometimes opens doors out of confining niches, and crossing those thresholds can be exhilarating, to put it mildly. For little Metex of Edison, New Jersey, fate came disguised as an irritated engineer from Ford Motor Co. in 1973, the year new emissions control laws mandated the use of catalytic converters on cars. As Metex Chairman Albert H. Cohen recalls it, the engineer informed him in the vernacular that Metex products didn't work on the Ford Pinto.

Al Cohen was mystified. Metex was born in the twenties as a producer of knitted-copper scouring pads and transformed in the fifties by then-owner General Cable into a producer of insulation for electronic devices. Metex, now independent again, had never sold anything to Ford, as far as Cohen knew. It turned out that the Ford technician was talking about custom-designed knitted wire mesh cradles Metex had made for Englehard Minerals to cradle catalytic converters on a factory forklift truck.

How on earth did that little thing get in the hands of Ford? Cohen wondered. But Cohen, who grew up fatherless and on welfare in New York's tough Bedford-Stuyvesant, still had enough street smarts to spot a main chance when he saw one. Who cared how Ford got hold of his wire products? Ford had to put millions of catalytic converters on its cars, and if it was interested enough to send a man out to complain about a Metex support that hadn't been designed for cars in the first place, Cohen had a first-class marketing opportunity disguised as a service complaint.

Here was a potential encore for Metex as accidental as Osborn's Ramron. But there were important differences. Osborn was far more profitable than Metex, which had been depleted by ill-advised mergers under Cohen's predecessor and still lacked the type of lucrative niches that Osborn enjoyed. Cohen was also nearly thirty years younger than Osborn's Smith, and he had a much smaller stake in a much less attractive company.

So Cohen took the plunge. Working day and night at Ford headquarters in Dearborn, Michigan, with his top engineers, Cohen—an analytical chemist by training—finally figured out how to redesign the Metex mesh cradle so that the converter wouldn't be blown out the tailpipe.

Result: Just before the Metex annual meeting Cohen found himself with the prospect of a $30 million order. To fill it he would have to invest twice the net worth of the company. But the auto companies offered little more than a handshake. None of them liked converters. They fervently hoped converters would go away and take the Metex cradle along with them.

Cohen decided to gamble anyway. "It's the kind of opportunity that I don't think will ever come again," he says. It was also an opportunity that could vanish at a moment's notice. So he moved as prudently as he could. Shortly after the plant was built with bank loans, Ford and Chrysler were sufficiently impressed by Cohen's sincerity to give him sole-source supplier contracts for the cradles. But Cohen knew how fickle Detroit can be. He wrote off the new plant and the equipment in three years flat—lest there be no more profits to write the investment off against. He pumped as much of the earnings from the auto supply plant into the rest of the business as he possibly could.

Despite a brief setback during the Arab oil embargo of 1974, Cohen by 1976 was sitting pretty. Earnings had gone from $370,000 to $2 million even after heavy depreciation charges for the new plant. Return on equity hit a stunning 41 percent.

But Wall Street wasn't impressed. Clearly Metex had a product that could easily be copied and undersold. And that is just what happened. Price-cutting competition slashed Metex earnings in half in 1978.

---

*Even on your biggest gamble you can protect yourself to an important extent—if you're willing to take the punishment to earnings.*

---

Belatedly, Cohen realized that he should have offered to share the wealth with other contractors through licensing arrangements. That is what the aerospace industry does routinely. That way Detroit wouldn't have worried about having just one supplier, a concern that dates back to Henry Ford. That way price-cutting competition would not have been as ruthless. "Licensing arrangements would at least have permitted us to keep a piece of the business, if only through royalties," Cohen now admits.

But Cohen had protected himself in another way that now paid off. Those profits poured back into his traditional business now yielded a modest encore: a gasket called Thermoseal. It stopped the leakage of exhaust gases at the point where the manifold and the exhaust pipe connected on front-wheel drive cars, and yielded a more efficient engine.

With new emission standards due out, Cohen figured he was on the recovery trail. But a more efficient ceramic gasket stole his thunder. Meanwhile Japanese cars had taken a quarter of the U.S. auto market. By 1982 Cohen was facing price-cutting competition, and his margins were barely 10 percent of what they had been back in 1976.

So he started cutting back. Some 40 percent of the Metex staff was fired, and one of its factories was shut down. The wire mesh electronic shielding business and the chemical process business were sold for a combined gain of close to $3.2 million. Then Cohen tried to acquire his way out of trouble. He bought a tiny parts supplier to the oilfield business just before that industry collapsed. "We sold it back to them in the fall 1984 and got out with our skins," says Cohen.

A better move occurred early in 1985 with the acquisition of an airborne antenna systems company for roughly $8 million in cash, stock, and notes. That company, Dynaport, will double Metex's size and put it at least into other, promising markets. "They make very high performance antennas for military aircraft and tactical satellite communications, which is very much the leading edge of that technology," says Cohen. "They're the world leader in that field. They are represented on every major military airframe. We were very fortunate that they decided to sell the business."

Meanwhile, thanks in large measure to the "voluntary" embargo on Japanese auto imports, Metex earnings have snapped back to slightly over 1979 levels. But price competition in catalytic converter supports finally drove Cohen out of that market. His biggest product now is Thermoseal. "We took the Thermoseal technology through four generations of product design," says Cohen. "And despite four domestic competitors and four European competitors we are now the largest supplier of Thermoseal gaskets in the world. It's a highly profitable line of business. In 1983 we returned about 45 percent on assets employed, and about 36 percent in 1984. We're introducing yet another generation of Thermoseal products that is going to strengthen our market share further, and we've started manufacturing in Europe as well."

That Cohen has been able to do as well as he has, finding niches in mass markets with low-technology products, is quite a tribute to his strategic skills and his determination.

"Looking back, I realize we weren't getting a real pay-back on the catalytic converter support profits that we reinvested in the rest of the business," says Cohen. "After Thermoseal, we really didn't get another big hit. It took us too long to recognize that we were running a maturing $14 million highly competitive business with twice the staff we needed. Our mistake was that we were following every in-dustrial application for our materials technology. There were always things in the mill that looked like they had po-tential. We didn't turn away any potential order that in-volved engineering development. That took a lot of bucks, and the source of funds for that had dried up. We should have scaled back sooner."

It's not easy to admit you are unable to create your own solution through new product development. But some-times, if you're alert, fate will intervene and give you a new lease on life as the Dynaport acquisition, like the catalytic support before it, did for Cohen.

# 36

## The False Health of a Withering Niche

You might argue that Al Cohen indirectly created his own opportunities in a low-technology business by designing that little specialty converter cradle for Englehard, or that Osborn did too, simply by upgrading its existing products. But there are some niches in which such product extension encores are quite a bit more difficult.

Take Chicago's Health-Mor, for example. Health-Mor makes vacuum cleaners that sell for seven hundred to eight hundred dollars apiece—a good ten times more than the average Hoover. With around three times the suction of ordinary vacuum cleaners, they are designed for the fastidious person who sincerely wants a rug *clean*. About 3 to 4 percent of the vacuum cleaner market is willing to pay a premium for that kind of suction.

By the end of the seventies, Health-Mor, with a respectable $27 million in sales, had racked up an average 25 percent return on equity over the preceding five years on no debt. This is no mean feat in a tough narrow-margin business that even General Electric couldn't make a go of. (GE sold out in 1972.)

Health-Mor looked like the classic "cash cow"—a company in a mature, slow-growing business generating more cash than it consumed. A cash cow is ideal for a leveraged

buyout by someone like Dermot Dunphey. It is also ideal as
a solid base from which to grow an acquisitions-oriented
company. In short, Health-Mor looked precisely like what
every young M.B.A. was supposed to be searching for as a
vehicle to make his fortune.

---

*A dead-end niche may be a cash cow. But trying to break
out of that niche can eat up that cash flow quickly and may
even hurt the core business.*

---

Enter a young man named John Licht, a former Price
Waterhouse C.P.A. who was Health-Mor's chief financial
officer. He took over from Chairman Albert F. Kramer, a
former salesman, on Kramer's death in September of 1981.
"In a three-and-a-half-year period we had three CEOs die,"
says Licht, by way of explaining how he wound up in the
top spot. Was it the opportunity of a lifetime? "We were in
big trouble, to be honest with you," he replies.

Trouble? With numbers like that, you'd think would-be
entrepreneurs would be lined up all the way to Cleveland
just for a chance to experience such "trouble."

"You could see the corner we were backing ourselves
into," Licht explains. "It was something I felt needed to be
changed for a long time but didn't have the authority. We
were losing our share of the market because we were trying
to serve two masters with the same product, and that's just
not possible. We were selling at retail the same product that
we were selling door-to-door."

The problem had started many years ago. For many
years a direct-sales (door-to-door) company, Health-Mor
suddenly found that market dwindling—as Fuller Brush
had many years before. To supplement flagging door-to-
door sales the company introduced the same high-priced
vacuum cleaner in retail stores.

But the strategy backfired badly. "The door-to-door people would generate the demand," says Licht. "Then, after our door-to-door man left, the customer would start calling around to the local retail stores and buy it there. Eventually that forced the door-to-door salesman out of business. Then retail sales fell off because there was no more demand created by the door-to-door man." In other words there was a cancer underneath that seeming glow of health in the Health-Mor numbers—a cancer very few outsiders, however experienced, would have been able to detect without considerable study.

Once detected, of course, there was a clear—if not exactly painless—solution: Put a different, lower-priced model into the retail stores and continue selling the high-priced model door-to-door. "It's an attempt to create another niche," says Licht.

Why didn't the high-priced model do well by itself in stores? "Our product was a high-priced item, and you have to demonstrate why they're worth as much as they're worth," Licht explains. "The retail salesman will not do that because a customer will come in, and he'll say, I want a vacuum cleaner, and the guy will say, 'Well, I've got one over here for $89 and one over here for $149 and one over here for $789,' and the customer will say, 'Well, let's look at these two over here' because they don't take the time to tell the story."

So in early 1982 Health-Mor came out with its knockoff. But it didn't help, because with a $550 price tag it suffered the same fate as the $789 machine. Then came the pain. "We literally canceled all our retail stores. Legally, you've got to make your marketing change affect everybody the same way. They weren't real happy about it, but nobody ever is when you take something away."

Health-Mor's return on equity sank to 7.7 percent in 1982 and 10.3 percent in 1983—a far cry from the late seventies. Licht knew that would happen, but had no choice.

"It's better that than extinction," he says crisply. Had his predecessors shied away from taking that step because it was obviously going to be painful? "I'm sure that's a large part of it," Licht replies. "But you take a fifty-eight-year-old company, and it's time to start reevaluating its future, not just looking at the day-to-day."

Factor in a 40 percent founding-family equity position in the stock, and you appreciate the courage of that decision a bit more.

Now Licht is trying to win back Health-Mor's former door-to-door men. "It's tough," he admits. "It certainly hasn't been easy. That kind of experience leaves a bad taste in their mouths."

Meanwhile, Health-Mor earnings in early 1985 showed a modest 7 percent increase. "That isn't anything to write home about," says Licht, "but we have a very large overseas customer who was 11 percent of our business last year and ordered exactly nothing in the first quarter of this year. I guess they got themselves financially backed up."

So the numbers don't always tell the story. Health-Mor never looked healthier than when it was being forced out of its niche in a disastrous new direction. It remains to be seen whether John Licht can find the right solution to a withering niche.

# 37

## The Right Stuff

Of course, there are always some in any crowd who make it all look easy. Among entrepreneurial companies, the Pall Corp. of Long Island, New York, makers of fine filters for aerospace, electronics, chemical, and pharmaceutical applications, has long seemed to have the right stuff. Its return on equity has risen from an impressive average of 22.3 percent in the late seventies to an outstanding 30 percent since then on very little debt and without the aid of any significant acquisitions.

What's the secret? Pall President Abraham Krasnoff likes to say it's having a genius like chairman and founder Dr. David P. Pall around to keep inventing encores. After all, it was Pall's pioneering work on the Manhattan Project that gave Pall Corp. its first product line in 1944: porous steel filters for corrosive chemicals.

But in a sense this is too facile an answer. Bright as Dr. Pall unquestionably is, there are countless other entrepreneurial companies that have been founded by people of exceptional intelligence but that have never even come close to matching Pall's superb track record.

In truth, Pall struggled hard to get where it is today. Back in 1964 Pall's growth came to an abrupt halt when its main aircraft market nosedived. It would be years before that industry recovered. By 1972, Pall looked as though it wasn't going to be around much longer. The company had been barely breaking even for eight years straight. Then Owens-Corning unexpectedly changed its method of making fiberglass, rendering the material unsuitable for Pall filters. So Pall was forced to borrow heavily to finance its own fiberglass plant. It also attempted to diversify into pumps and airborne air-conditioning systems, but with little success. Pall, which had sold for as much as sixty times earnings in years past, now looked like a flash in the pan.

But appearances were deceiving. It turned out the reason Pall had fared so poorly in its attempted diversification was that the company's driving force, Dr. Pall, was busy working on something else: a new type of disposable filter. Having been technically outflanked in porous steel filters for the chemical industry, Pall was determined not to let that happen to the cloth and woven wire mesh filters he had developed to keep airborne dust out of jet engines. He discovered that a filter for the job could be made out of paper, epoxy resin, and very fine fiberglass fibers.

So while Abe Krasnoff and his management team were trying to diversify out of their niche in exactly the way any textbook would recommend, the founder and soul of the company was sticking to filters. And filters was where it was to be for Pall.

---

*When you've got a technical genius, bet on him, but be sure to get him to focus on market problems.*

---

As any venture capitalist will tell you, there are many different ways to build a successful business. The hard part is to find which way most closely meshes with the entrepreneur's own particular skills and personality.

Krasnoff, a consummate pragmatist, will only say that if Dr. Pall had been persuaded to focus on pumps or air-conditioning systems, then the company might have turned out to have a very different product mix. But one does not tell Dr. Pall what to do, says Krasnoff, a C.P.A. who back in the forties came to help out a neighbor with his accounting and stayed to become head of the neighbor's company. Krasnoff soon discovered that working shoulder-to-shoulder with a genius, even if he happens to be your neighbor, can be demanding. "If you are going to get along with a genius," Krasnoff says, "you need some of the attributes of a chameleon, and some of an antelope."

The first lesson was that he was generally better off working with the genius rather than against him. "We discovered that we weren't really smart enough, without Dr. Pall, to solve other people's unsolved technical problems," says Krasnoff. "But we also discovered that there were really broad opportunities for disposable filters. It was just a question of moving from dumb to smarter.

"We discovered that if we moved slightly beyond filtration into the removal of contaminants from liquids and gases we would be a company that was three inches high in technology—very narrowly oriented in fluid clarification—and fifty miles wide in our markets," Krasnoff says. "We'd look in one direction and find a hospital market. We'd look in another direction and find machine tools."

Many businessmen would find such a narrow presence in so many markets a recipe for disaster. The cost of carving out tiny niches in many vastly different markets could prove ruinous.

But this is only partly true, Krasnoff discovered. "It's costly not so much to find the niches as to find a way to market to them," he explains. "The solution dawned on me many years ago: We had to find independent, technically trainable, entrepreneurially run distributors who knew the market section we wanted to reach. Having found the market ourselves, we would then develop a product for it and usually make the first sales. Then we'd find distributors who were already serving that market with related products."

Pall monitors its many distributors closely with one administrator for every seven distributors, plus a technical support team. Each narrow market has its own self-contained organization. "If I organize a narrowly oriented marketing effort, I can, with good management, beat superior people who have more complex management structures. My narrowly oriented people can learn their market better than somebody with a lot of complexity."

Like the fledgling English navy in Elizabethan England battling the Spanish Armada in the storm-tossed Channel, victory goes to the speedy and the agile in a confined space. The operative word is *confined.* Just as the faster, lighter British boats would have been blown out of the water in the open ocean, so would Pall have come a cropper in a broader market. It's the wise admiral who forces the battle on waters of his own choosing.

Over time there's an additional advantage: Because Pall is so focused and has so much proprietary knowledge in its field, competition is less of a problem. That means distributors can charge more for Pall products than they can on most of the distributors' lines and record fatter margins. That means more profit to the distributors, who tend to pay more and more attention to the Pall product line.

"You don't avoid imitation," says Krasnoff. "You keep advancing technology. And here, there are three basic lessons: One is you never underestimate the competition. The second is you always stay in close touch with the leading-edge customers so you're abreast of their perception of the major technologies. And the third is to be the one who advances the technology."

But what happens when Pall saturates each of its small niches? "You have to keep developing new opportunities,"

Krasnoff says. "Our perception is that we ought to grow at 15 to 20 percent with normal price increases and when currency problems aren't depressing us. About 40 percent of our sales are overseas. As long as the total market available for the products we sell is about ten times our present size, we feel we can grow at our usual rate. And we keep assessing that in each of our markets. Our oldest market, for example, has a market potential that is only five times our present size. We try to develop other markets to expand on our old one. For example, for the military we are now developing the nuclear, biological, chemical warfare protection area.

"The lesson we learned is that you have to find your niche and keep developing your expertise in it in a market-driven way. That's the key."

How do you harness a mind like Dr. Pall's to market demand? The literature on research and development can cite innumerable examples of how counterproductive it is to chain scientists to the marketing department.

Abe Krasnoff has a very simple answer to that one. Tap the entrepreneurial instinct in research people. Says Krasnoff: "Dr. Pall is intelligent, so it doesn't take a lot of persuasion. In addition to being a genius, he's a very bright fellow!"

The rest, as they say, is history.

# 38

## Après Moi . . . Passing the Baton

If entrepreneurs weren't absolutely convinced that theirs was the one true vision of commercial success, they wouldn't have the nerve to start companies in the first place. So one of the classic problems successful entrepreneurial companies encounter in trying to find an encore is grooming a replacement for the founder. Successful entrepreneurs, deservedly proud of their own courage, often have a hard time handing over the reins to someone else who has not yet demonstrated that same courage. How many companies have been sold simply because the founder never bothered to groom a successor or wouldn't let him take the helm or actually sabotaged him?

---

*Passing the baton is one of the toughest problems there is for entrepreneurs. They know how hard it was for them.*

---

Consider the case of Waters Associates, the world leader in liquid chromatography equipment. Liquid chromatography is a process for analyzing or purifying complex chemical compounds.

Waters started as a company in search of a mission. "I started with five employees in 1958," says founder Jim Waters. "We were some good people looking for a market. I started out thinking that developing instruments for other people was a good idea."

Venture capitalists are generally quite skeptical of such a strategy. But Waters had confidence in his own abilities as an inventor. Soon he had designed a new type of refractometer, which opened up a number of possible markets. Waters began to define the company mission more narrowly.

"We decided to get into process control instruments. In time we did some work for Dow Chemical and licensed their gel permeation chromatography technology in 1963. On the basis of that we grew very rapidly. We began developing the skills that related to general liquid chromatography although we had great doubt as to whether liquid chromatography would really go anyplace. Since diffusion in liquids is ten thousand times slower than diffusion in gases, people always thought liquid chromatography would be far slower than gas chromatography."

That's the kind of assumption an inventor/entrepreneur loves to challenge. He is motivated in part by an iconoclastic attitude and a fair amount of egotism. Perhaps it's that willingness to challenge accepted ideas that makes entrepreneurs so "difficult" or "different"—and so important.

At this point, Waters Associates, a marginal operation from the start, was hurt badly by the recession of 1970. It had to sell some stock to nearby Millipore—a high-tech filtration company that would have preferred to buy Waters outright, at least at that point.

Millipore quickly spotted the need for someone like Abe Krasnoff to take charge of day-to-day management at Waters while Waters acted like Dr. Pall. It brought in Frank Zenie, an engineer from neighboring Foxboro Controls. Zenie, a hard-nosed corporate executive, soon laid off over a quarter of the employees, saying the company was trying to do too many things at once.

"I never wanted to be just a manager," says Waters. "So in the beginning I managed the thing as if it were just a big project, which is rather typical of us entrepreneurs. I realized I had to delegate. Some of my recruits worked out well. Others didn't. Frank was my vice-president of manufacturing, and it soon became very clear to me that Frank was outstanding.

"I agreed I was trying to do too much," Waters says. "Frank and I got along well right up to maybe 1976. I turned over the presidency to Frank in about 1971, and we killed about half of the research projects. It was really Frank's leadership that did it. I probably wouldn't have done it by myself. He showed me we were better off concentrating on a few things and doing them well."

That cannot have been an easy lesson for Waters, who had survived hand-to-mouth for years as an entrepreneurial engineer of all trades.

By the midseventies, it was clear that Zenie and Waters were not seeing eye-to-eye, despite the fact the company was showing a stunning 27 percent return on equity with very little debt against competition from the likes of du Pont, Hewlett-Packard, and Perkin Elmer. Astute investors might have suspected this from the fact that Millipore had by this point sold off its Waters Associates position.

"We were growing 40 percent a year, and after four years of that growth you don't have enough middle management," says Waters. "It was an interesting thing; Frank was very good at running a company where the key players were in place, and he could optimize their performance. Eventually, the directors said to Frank, 'You've got to add more people.' "

The company was literally choking on business at that point, says Waters: "I think Frank didn't anticipate the lead time that's required to get people to be productive. And he began to behave as if he ought to be treated as the founder—that Jim Waters ought to be put on the sidelines."

Waters was looking for trouble now. Eventually Zenie added more people but didn't train them adequately, he says. "By 1978 our research had practically failed. Our key guy was put on the shelf by Frank for two years so another guy could take over the research effort. Frank's idea was if you hire a guy, you've got to let him do the job and remove the impediments, rather than saying the guy has a function with the culture as it is. So we just got no products out for two years."

---

*Entrepreneurs can begin to dislike their appointed successors, even to the point of trying to ensure that they fail.*

---

Waters became increasingly concerned and told the directors that something had to be done. But he adds quickly: "I was not suggesting that I ought to take over because I really wasn't the guy to do it."

By mid-1979 the directors told Frank to concentrate on long-run strategy and let another man take over as chief operating officer. I thought that was a really good move. Unfortunately [the new man] was not strong enough to stand up to Frank."

Was Waters part of the problem? Saying that he wanted to give Zenie a free hand, Waters, with all his concerns about the company, was only dropping by the office once a week at this point. The directors were confused. Who was really in charge? Waters had the control block of stock and the chairman's title. But Zenie was the chief executive.

Says Waters: "I finally just told the directors that my 29 percent of the stock had the power of merger and that once the company had another owner, the owner would do the right thing. Millipore at that point was not my prime candidate. I was thinking of IBM."

Zenie and his chief operating officer said they would quit unless Waters merged with Millipore, which understood the business well and knew its people.

"D'Arbeloff [Millipore's chairman] has always been a good friend of mine," says Waters. "So I said as long as they make a reasonable offer, it's all right with me."

Millipore did make a reasonable offer and bought Waters. "Unfortunately, Millipore's earnings turned down within six months of the time we merged," says Waters. "Millipore evaluated Zenie and moved him out to a strategy role. Then they replaced Frank's chief operating officer with a manager of theirs, Gary Frazier, who did a beautiful job of restoring morale. After six months, Zenie and his former number two man left and founded a company that makes robotic sample handling equipment for laboratories." The bitterness toward Zenie is still evident. Waters charges that Zenie stole a lot of Waters' employees.

Once he'd sold Waters Associates, Waters served on the Millipore board for four years. But a life of leisure was not for him. "I finally realized that my heart was more with the small enterprise than it was with the big one," he says.

So he went back to being an entrepreneur again. He started investing in a number of companies and started a computer software company called Waters Business Systems—a marketing system that keeps track of sales calls, literature requests, and service calls on equipment in the field. Now that his no-compete clause with Millipore has expired, he recently invested in a small company in Pittsburgh doing "supercritical chromatography."

"It's not much competition to Millipore anyway," he says. "It's a group of ten young guys in Pittsburgh who remind me a lot of myself when I was thirty years old. It's kind of nice to tell them 'watch out for this one' or 'that's a technique that worked for me.'"

Could Waters Associates have survived as an independent entity? "I think it could have," says Waters. "I think we would have been a little bit better off if we had survived as an independent company. I guess my biggest regret is that I lost control. I had the philosophy that the board of directors ought to be independent people who really thought about the problems, and that may have been a mistake in the sense that I didn't pack the board with my cronies. So when the chips come down, there's always the fear that the entrepreneur is a bit of a madman. And I understand that, and I just wasn't able to convince them that I really wasn't a madman and that they really needed to take action."

# 39
## The Path Finder

Experienced entrepreneurs, who know they want to be professional pathfinders always starting new companies, face
an interesting dilemma in the computer business where two
years is a long time: What do you write in the business plan
you show the venture capitalists? Do you tell them that
even though you're in your forties and the company doesn't
exist yet, you plan to resign as chief executive in, say, five
years?

Well, that's exactly what happened at Apollo Computer.
With sales of $216 million and an extraordinary price-earn-
ings multiple of sixty plus, four-year-old Apollo looked hot
in 1985. Its scientific and engineering work stations, which
can link to an office network, have superior three-dimen-
sional graphics and software for project work that needs to
be passed back and forth quickly between many people.

*One way to make sure you pass the baton in time is to get
into a fast-moving business and then make a specialty of
successful start-ups.*

Anyone familiar with the track records of Apollo's top
executives would have predicted a bright future for the new
company. Chairman and Chief Executive John William
Poduska had been research head and one of the seven

founders of Prime Computer. He brought with him as co-founders two other top Prime executives, two Digital Equipment men, and two Data General men—plus a finance man from outside the industry. Most of them were in their forties and experienced with the problems start-up companies can face in the computer business.

But in October of 1984, forty-seven-year-old Poduska stepped down as chief executive in favor of Thomas Vanderslice, who had recently lost a management succession battle at GTE, and before that had been top contender to succeed Reginald Jones as chief executive of General Electric.

Why would an entrepreneur as successful as Poduska engineer his own retirement as chief executive at forty-seven? His venture capitalists couldn't have been more enthusiastic about Apollo under his management.

He says he left because he's never run a billion-dollar company and Vanderslice has. The only way to stay on top of the competition in as fast-paced a field as Apollo's is to outgrow it, he goes on, and at its current rate, Apollo will do a billion in sales by 1987. Poduska, who feels he is best at starting up new companies, has gone on to launch another one in a related field.

When an entrepreneur includes in his business plan a clause predicting his own retirement in four or five years' time, as Poduska did with Apollo Computer, a new era of entrepreneur as company-starting specialist may well have dawned.

# 40
## One More Time!

The first thing to remember about repeating your initial success as an entrepreneur is that you really don't have to. There is absolutely nothing wrong with cashing in your chips. You may have exhausted all the permutations of that original idea, as Godley and Reed did at Xomox. Ask yourself how many corporate executives would be proud to have demonstrated just once that they, too, were true entrepreneurs the way you have done?

If you do decide to try again, remember that you don't literally have to repeat your first success: That is, you don't have to invent another new product yourself.

You can acquire it. Think of Lee Rizzuto of Conair acquiring Jherri Redding as a fallback while he tried to invent his way out of Conair problems. The Redding acquisition proved to be a godsend. Al Cohen of Metex found a new beginning in an acquisition after he was priced out of his initial innovation in woven wire mesh. But neither of those lifesaving acquisitions would have been possible without that first entrepreneurial success that established Conair and Metex as formidable innovators and companies that knew how to manage growth.

Then there's Dermot Dunphey of Sealed Air, whose strategy from the outset was to acquire a series of related niches, a proven formula.

There are new hurdles to leap when you search for an encore. You have to be capable of managing change by attracting superior people the way that Ted Schad of Lou-Ana Foods has done, for example.

There are even times when the opportunity or invention that could open up major future markets for your company comes at the wrong time. It came too late, for example, for Norm Smith of Osborn Manufacturing. While Al Cohen of Metex was young enough to accept the challenge of a growth opportunity that almost entailed betting the company on it, Norm Smith was not.

Some companies, like Pall Corp., are lucky enough to have inventive geniuses on staff who really are worth betting the company on for the needed encores, provided one makes sure the inventor is always focused on the right market.

Perhaps the most critical part of building a company that will last longer than you do is passing the baton to the next generation of leaders. That can be one of the hardest tasks an entrepreneur ever has to face. Only a few entrepreneurs, like Ted Schad of Lou-Ana Foods, eventually see that delegation and nurturing the creative spirit in others is for them the truest fulfillment of entrepreneurship.

# Index

247

M L